Amiga A600
Insider Guide

Amiga A600
Insider Guide

An Introduction to Workbench and AmigaDOS on the A600 and A600HD

Bruce Smith

Bruce Smith Books

© Bruce Smith 1992
ISBN: 1-873308-14-0
First Edition: December 1992.

Editors: Mark Webb, Peter Fitzpatrick
Typesetting: Bruce Smith Books Ltd

Workbench, Amiga and AmigaDOS are trademarks of Commodore-Amiga, Inc. UNIX is a trademark of AT&T. MS-DOS is a trademark of Microsoft Corporation. Designer Mouseware is a trademark of Mark Smiddy. All other Trademarks and Registered Trademarks used are hereby acknowledged.

Disclaimer: While every effort has been made to ensure that the information in this publication (and any programs and software) is correct and accurate, the Publisher can accept no liability for any consequential loss or damage, however caused, arising as a result of using the information printed in this book.

E & OE

Bruce Smith Books is an imprint of Bruce Smith Books Limited.

Published by: Bruce Smith Books Limited. PO Box 382, St. Albans, Herts, AL2 3JD. Telephone: (0923) 894355, Fax: (0923) 894366.

Registered in England No. 2695164.

Registered Office: 51 Quarry Street, Guildford, Surrey, GU1 3UA.

Printed and bound in the UK by Ashford Colour Press, Gosport.

The Author

BRUCE SMITH is an award winning journalist with over 40 book titles to his credit. His style is renowned for being easy going and highly readable and led one reviewer to write *"This is the first computer book I have read in bed for pleasure rather than to cure insomnia!"*

In addition to the computer scene, he is well known as a football journalist and his dulcet tones can generally be heard on *BBC Radio Bedfordshire with Herts and Bucks* on Saturday afternoons.

He is the founder of Bruce Smith Books, a publishing house dedicated to the support of the Amiga, and lives in rural Hertfordshire. He is married with two children and his hobbies include amateur dramatics and scuba diving.

Contents

Appendices

Insider Guides

The Amiga A600 is an amazing computer. If you are
wondering if, and indeed why, you should fork out
some more cash for a book, don't read on.

Then again if you want to get the very best from
your Amiga you had really better read on...

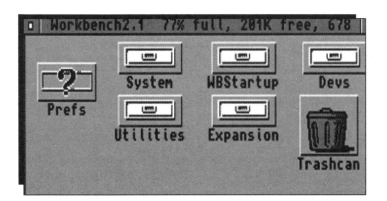

Y ou will be reading this either in the comfort of your own
home or standing in a shop wondering if you should,
after having shelled out a few hundred quid already,
fork out some more portraits of Charles Dickens for this book.
If you are the former then you will have already decided why
you should make it your computing companion. If you are in
the latter category read on and I'll tell you why *you* should.

The bottom line is that this book has been written with the first
time user in mind, what's more it has been written specifically
with the first time user of the A600 or A600HD in mind.

The manual supplied with the computer is a comprehensive
description of what your new computer has to offer and it contains within its pages details on virtually all aspects of the
Workbench (that's the bit of the computer that you will initially
be using the most).

This book does not cover every aspect of your Amiga, it will not
make you into an instant Amiga expert – that only comes with

a lot of personal research and endeavour. However, what this book will do is to take you step by step through all the major areas that you must know about if you are to use you Amiga effectively and make the very best of your investment. It will in effect be a *guide* to the Amiga in the real sense of the word.

The ultimate aim of this book then is to provide you with a thorough grounding in the main aspects of the A600 – to get you inside it – from which point you should then be able to master it using either your own initiative or one of the sister publications covering all aspects of the Amiga. This *Insider Guide* will provide the basis from which you will feel comfortable to go to and use your Amiga A600 manual to extract any extra information you need with confidence.

To make this progress I would ask of you just one thing. Start at Chapter One and read through the book – don't jump chapters – and do work through the tutorials provided. When you have tried out the examples, do another of your own. Apply your new found knowledge, make mistakes (and you will) and learn from them.

Okay, that's the sales pitch. If you're reading this at home – thanks and good luck with your endeavours – don't be frightened to experiment. If you're in the shop and still undecided – I must be losing my touch!

Setting the scene – This *Insider Guide* covers both the A600 and A600HD versions of the Amiga. What's the difference between them and is one better than the other?

Sorting out your disks and getting up and running is not that confusing – is it?

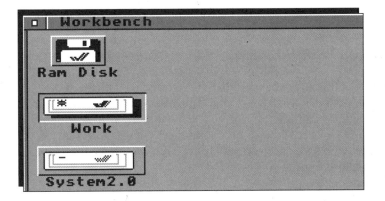

*I*f you have read the adverts and reviews or have had some good sales advice in the shop you will already be aware that the A600 comes in two flavours – plain vanilla (that's the A600 itself) and raspberry ripple (that's the more expensive and slightly more tasty A600HD). Fundamentally the A600 and the A600HD are one and the very same – they run the same software – but HD stands for Hard Disk and that's what you get for your extra cash: a hard disk fitted internally.

Although both the A600 and A600HD run the same software – the inclusion of a hard disk does drastically increase the functionality of the computer because it means you have virtually instant access to all your software.

The alternative to a hard disk is a floppy disk which is the basic building block of computer data storage and transfer the world over. All Amigas are fitted with an internal 3.5" floppy disk drive, located on the right hand edge of the machine. We'll come onto the technicalities on what a floppy disk is capable of storing in due course, but if we say that the A600HD hard disk can store around twenty times as much information as a single floppy disk you should begin to get an inkling of how useful and how time saving this might be. In essence you won't need to swap disks at regular intervals.

But, having said that – don't start fretting if you have a floppy disk based A600 only – these will be the most popular of all the A600 sold and they are just as sophisticated as their counterparts – and you also have the option of purchasing an add-on drive at a later date as and when they become available from third-party suppliers. A word for A600HD users as well – you also have a floppy disk drive fitted into the side of your Amiga.

I have flipped between descriptions of the A600 and A600HD with regularity so far. Don't be put off by this because it won't happen that much more. The reason being is that the software on both machines is the same. Both run Workbench and AmigaDOS and for that reason the descriptions and tutorials for both are identical! Wherever minor differences do occur I'll be sure to point them out – but they are few and far between and, once you have set up your system to your liking, they virtually disappear.

Versions

Having said that the A600 comes in two flavours it also comes into a couple of different wrappings in terms of the software supplied with the machine. If you brought your machine after the Autumn of 1992 it is likely that you will be supplied with version 2.1 of Workbench. Prior to this it may well be Workbench 2.04 or 2.05. The simplest way to find out is to pick up and look at the label on the Workbench disk. If it says Workbench 2.1 then you have, not surprisingly Workbench 2.1. If on the other hand it says Workbench 2.0 then you will be using version 2.04 (A600) or version 2.05 (A600HD).

In terms of differences there is not a great deal. Basically version 2.1 provides some extras in terms of utilities. It has also been upgrade a little in the way that information is presented on screen. Additionally the positioning of the software across a couple of the disks has been rearranged. All that said in terms of you actually using the software very little has changed. I'll concentrate on both versions through this Insider Guide and also point out where things are different when necessary. Provided you know what version of Workbench you are using you should not notice any real difference!

Floppy Disks

No matter whether you have an A600 or an A600HD you will find that your Amiga pack has a set of floppy disks, the master disks. This are very important so treat them with respect. If you are an A600 user then these will form the focal point of your attention for the rest of this book. If you have a hard disk system then you can put them away somewhere safe as the programs and information they contain is already in position on the hard disk – but more on that later.

The disks are labelled:

Workbench

Extras

Fonts

Under Workbench 2.1 there is an extra disk called:

Locale

and, if you have an A600HD there is one extra disk:

A600HD Install Disk

We'll look at this in greater detail shortly, but first...Setting up!

Setting Up

I'm not going to waste precious space going through how to connect up your Amiga. The reason being is that it is done beautifully in the small booklet entitled *Introducing the A600* which is supplied in your Amiga box. The whole caboodle is remarkably easy to plug together and it is physically impossible to plug the wrong plug into the wrong socket and blow the thing up, so rest assured!

A600: When you turn this on your screen will show an animated cartoon of a disk flying up and inserting itself in a disk drive. This is the A600's way of asking you to insert the Workbench disk into the internal floppy disk drive. Locate the disk called Workbench and pop it into the drive (Workbench title facing upwards and metal slider innermost). Within a handful of seconds a screen called KeyMap Selection will appear.

A600HD: When you switch on the A600 will go through its starting up procedure the technical term for this being booting or kickstarting (basically the terms relate to be booted into life or kickstarted into action). This all takes a few seconds but within a few moments you will be presented with a screen that is headed KeyMap Selection.

KeyMap Select

The Amiga is an international computer. That is great but in itself it also creates an awful lot of problems – not least those encountered by the language barrier. For example, although English and German may be reasonably closely related the German language has many characters not included in the English alphabet.

It is reasonable to expect that an English Amiga would have an English keyboard and a German Amiga a German one. To enable this to happen the Amiga is supplied with a map of each of the major keyboard configurations, English, German, French, Swedish and several more. This keymap is not a map in the traditional sense but a set of numbers that reflect the keyboard characters. Before you set off into the world of Amiga you need to install the correct keymap (GB if you are a UK user). This is an area which has changed between Workbench versions 2.1 and 2.04/2.05.

That said at this point only A600HD users should do this. The reason being is the A600 users must first make back up copies of their master disks. Therefore if you are using a floppy disk based system only press the Return key to by-pass the KeyMap Selection screen should it present itself to you..

If you are an A600HD user, look down the list you will see that the British keyboard (gb) is number 8. Locate the 8 key on the keyboard, press it once and then press the Return key. This installs the correct keyboard map on your A600.

Again, this process only takes a few seconds and shortly thereafter you will be presented with the Workbench.

The Workbench

The Workbench: Once your Amiga, be it an A600 or A600HD has finished its start-up or boot procedure you will be presented with the *Workbench*. The Workbench provides you with an environment where you can do all your day-to-day tasks such as running games, application programs and copying disks to name but three. The Workbench is itself a program that runs in the Amiga with the sole aim in life of providing you with a *user-friendly* (ie simple to use) interface with the A600.

The term Workbench is a good one because that is exactly how you should treat it – a screen version of a work area where you do all of your computing. For this reason Workbench is sometimes referred to as the *Desktop*

The Workbench displays several features which characterise it, many of these you will learn about during the course of this Insider Guide, however the most major characteristic of the Workbench is that it is a *WIMP* system. The term is WIMP is an acronym which stands for: Windows, Icons, Pointers and Menus.

The Workbench is itself a window and it exhibits all of the qualities of the many other windows you will be encountering in the coming chapters – all of which will be fully described. A computer window works very much like a normal house window – you look through it (or into it) and see what it reveals on the other side. The larger the window the more you can see, the smaller the window the less you can see. A window only allows you to see part of the world, it doesn't show you everything (though it could if you made it big enough) as there may be items outside the area of view covered by the window. All these facts are true of household windows, they are also true of the Amiga Workbench windows.

The Menus

While Window puts the W into WIMP, Menus supplies the M. All Amiga menus are accessed via a menu bar that invariably sits across the top of the screen. When you are working at the Workbench then you will easily see the Workbench menu bar strung across the top of the Workbench screen.

In addition to displaying the version of Workbench you are using it also displays a number which represents the amount of memory that is available to you and your programs. This number will vary depending on whether you have had a memory upgrade fitted to your A600 or not.

The P in WIMP is for Pointer and the pointer is the arrow that you can move around the Workbench by moving the mouse across the table surface. The pointer will move in the direction your move the mouse.

If you move the Pointer so that its tip sits over the word Workbench and then press (and keep pressing) the right mouse button the Workbench changes and reveals some new legend – these are the names of the Workbench menus and they are Workbench, Window, Icons and Tools. If you move the pointer across each of these in turn you will find that a list of menu *options* pops down under each one.

Note that these pop-down menus only remain visible while you keep the mouse button depressed, when you release the button the pull-down menu disappears until recalled in similar fashion.

Selecting a Workbench menu option is relatively straightforward and really just requires some coordination between mouse and eye. For instance if you move the mouse to the menu bar, press down the right mouse button and move over the Workbench menu option you'll see that the first option on the menu is Backdrop. Move the pointer so that its point sits over the word Backdrop – you should notice that the option becomes *highlighted* – now release the mouse button. All being well you should have now selected the Backdrop option and the effect of this should be to turn or convert the Workbench from a window into a non-window environment called a Backdrop. If this hasn't happened then try the process again. You can return the Workbench to a Window by repeating the process, ie, select Backdrop again. It's worth practicing this a few times as menu selection is an important part of using your Amiga.

If you hadn't already guessed from above the I in WIMP stands for Icons. These are the small picture images that will appear on your Workbench and in windows that you open. You will be able to see a couple of icons on your desktop already – the Ram Disk is one and also the Workbench disk – if you are a A600HD user the latter will be replaced by a System and Work icon. More on icons in the next chapter.

Mouse Matters

If you don't already own one, then you will find a mouse mat a worthwhile investment. Table and desk tops tend to be slippery and offer the roller ball fitted in the base of the mouse no real surface to grip on and roll. A mouse mat is specially designed for use with a mouse and it also ensures that you keep a bit of the desk free for its use. Mouse mats vary in cost and dearest isn't always best. Always try any mouse mat out before you buy it.

Get into the habit of mouse-lift and move. You don't need an entire desktop to move the mouse around on – a small mouse mat is ample room. Simply push the mouse to its edge, lift and replace it on the opposite side of the mat, before continuing movement. It soon becomes a natural process.

To use the mouse effectively place it to the right of the Amiga with its tail (the wire) running away from you. Lay the palm of your hand over it with your index finger on the left button and your middle finger on the right hand button. This assumes you are right-handed like me! Obviously if you are left handed you will need to reverse these arrangements.

The left mouse button is the one which is used most so when you need to use the mouse button, press the left one unless you are told otherwise. Because the lefthand mouse button is used to select items it is often referred to as the Select button. The righthand mouse button is often called the Menu button as it is used to make the menus popdown.

Windows, Icons, Menus and Pointers – the Amiga WIMP building blocks.

Having introduced each of these in the last chapter, let's now look at the anatomy and physiology of each. Scalpels at the ready please!

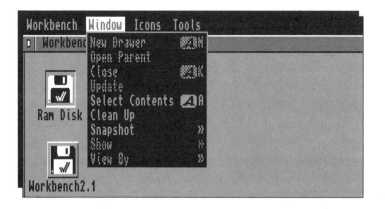

*A*ll windows on the Amiga exhibit similar characteristics, a fact which makes them very easy to use because, once you have learnt how to use one, you have also learnt how to use every other one!

The Workbench is by default a window but does differ in one respect from other windows in that you wouldn't really want to close it otherwise you'll be left with nothing to work on or with! So to that end it's best to experiment with another window and the best one for that purpose is the Workbench disk window.

If you are using an A600HD system then for the following you could insert the Workbench disk itself or pretend that the System2.1 icon on the Workbench is the disk icon in question.

At the moment the Workbench disk is represented by a disk icon (ie a cartoon of a disk with some legend underneath it). You can reveal its components by moving the pointer over it and then clicking the left mouse button twice in quick succession. This process is called *double-clicking*.

At this point the disk drive should spring into life and soon the Pointer will metamorphose into a small clock indicating to you that your keyboard has gone to sleep while the disk is being read – in other words while information or data is being located on it. If this does not happen then you have probably not double-clicked the mouse button quickly enough, or you haven't positioned the Pointer correctly over the disk icon. Try again. When you are successful the Workbench disk window will appear on the screen and then various icons will be displayed inside it.

Once the window has opened you will see that it becomes filled with a number of different icons each representing the various files that are held on the disk and which go towards the total working environment of the Workbench.

If you study the physical structure of the window you should see that it is composed of a number of elements, all of which are also reflected in the Workbench window. These elements, often called *gadgets* in Amiga parlance. From the top righthand corner, these are:

- Close gadget
- Title/Move Bar
- Zoom gadget
- Front/Back gadget
- Scroll gadgets
- Sizing gadget

Each of these is described individually below.

Close Gadget

The small square gadget with a white dot inside it situated in the very top lefthand corner of the window is the Close Window gadget. As its name suggests this is used to close the current window, effectively removing it from the Workbench screen. To use this gadget, position the tip of the Pointer so that it lies over the white dot and click on the mouse. The window will disappear from the screen. You can reopen the window again at any time simply by double-clicking again on the relevant icon. Try this a few times to get used to the process as it is a fundamental operation in the running of your Amiga Workbench.

Insider Guide #1: Disk icons give disk windows.

The Workbench disk appears as a named disk icon on the Workbench desktop. If you move the Pointer tip so that it sits anywhere over the disk icon and press the left mouse button twice in rapid succession (double-clicking) the Workbench disk window will be displayed. Note that the disk icon remains in place.

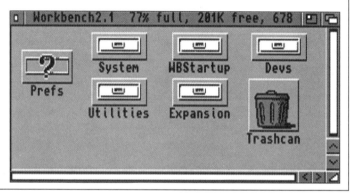

Insider Guide #2: The world of window gadgets.

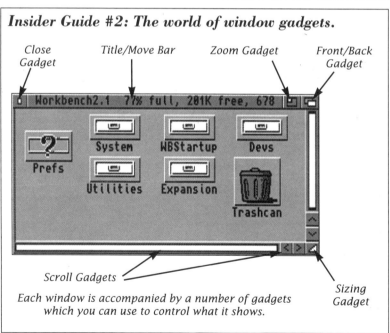

Each window is accompanied by a number of gadgets which you can use to control what it shows.

Title/Move Bar

The most readily distinguishable of the windows features, it runs almost right across the top of the window and is sandwiched in between the Close gadget and the Zoom gadget. The Title/Move bar contains details about the disk and also allows you to move the window around the desktop.

When a window is opened it will always display its name in the Title/Move Bar. This will generally be the same as the name assigned to the icon you used to open the window in the first place. The window name provides a useful point of reference which becomes important when you have several windows open on the Workbench at once.

The bar also contains information relating to the physical contents of the disk, namely the number of files on the disk and the amount of free space it contains. This free space size is important as it gives you an indication as to the amount of information that can be stored on it.

You can also use the bar to move the window around the desktop. This is done by positioning the Pointer anywhere within the bar and depressing the left mouse button. While keeping the mouse button depressed, when you move the mouse the window will be dragged around the Workbench in the same direction! Releasing the mouse button fixes the new window position until you reposition it once again. Try this with the Workbench disk window and notice that you are only dragging the outline of the window about, the window itself doesn't move until you release the mouse button.

Zoom Gadget

This gadget, which is immediately to the right of the Title/Move bar allows you to change the size of the window. The action of the gadget is to switch between two sizes. Generally, if a window is small when you open it, clicking on the double gadget will make it large. Clicking on the gadget again will restore the original window size.

Front/Back

In the far top righthand corner of the window is the Front/Back gadget. This has a dual action. If you have several windows open on screen at once then the Workbench can become a very cluttered place. Windows will generally overlap one another, partially obscuring the contents of the others around them. When you

Insider Guide #3: Shrinking and enlarging windows.

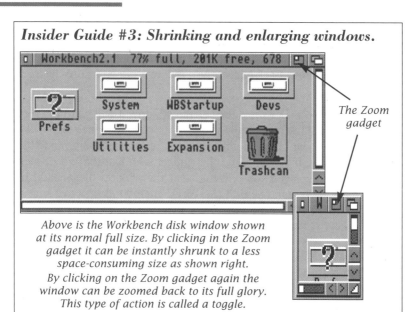

The Zoom gadget

Above is the Workbench disk window shown at its normal full size. By clicking in the Zoom gadget it can be instantly shrunk to a less space-consuming size as shown right.

By clicking on the Zoom gadget again the window can be zoomed back to its full glory. This type of action is called a toggle.

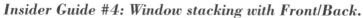

Insider Guide #4: Window stacking with Front/Back.

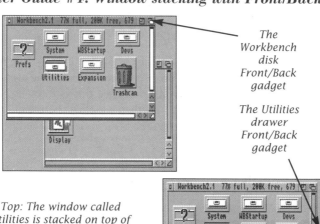

The Workbench disk Front/Back gadget

The Utilities drawer Front/Back gadget

Top: The window called Utilities is stacked on top of the Workbench disk window. To bring the Workbench disk window to the front (bottom) click on the Front/Back gadget in the Workbench disk window.

have several windows open they are said to be stacked. The topmost window, which is called the current window is by definition in the foreground. All other windows are in the background. By clicking the Pointer on the Front/Back gadget the window is either sent to the back or brought to the front.

If the window you click on is the current window it will go to the very bottom of the stack of windows. Any other window which is not the current window will be brought to the top of the stack and made the current window. If you click on this gadget with just the Workbench disk window displayed you will find that the window disappears! In fact it has simply gone behind the Workbench window – to bring it back click in the Workbench window's own Front/Back gadget!

Scroll Bars

Because it is possible to make a window smaller, there may be occasions when it is simply too small to show you all the icons it contains. Equally, you may have so many icons in a window that there isn't enough room to make the window big enough to show all the icons! This is where the scroll bars come into play. The scroll bars are located across the bottom and down the righthand edge of the window – they are therefore normally referred to as the horizontal scroll bar and the vertical scroll bar.

The Scroll Bars are held within the Scroll Boxes. By dragging the Scroll Bars inside their Scroll Boxes you can make other areas of the window come into view. The best way to see this is to make the window about half its present size and then practice the technique. The window can be made smaller using the Sizer gadget detailed next.

An alternative method is to click the Pointer over the arrow gadgets which will force the window to scroll the icons and shift their positions in the direction indicated by the arrow head.

Window Sizer

When you open a window it is displayed in a predetermined size. However, you will invariably wish to alter the size, making it either larger of smaller. The Window Sizer gadget allows you to do this.

You use this gadget in much the same way as you would do the Move Window gadget. Place the Pointer over the gadget, keep the left mouse button depressed and then drag the Pointer. You can perform the drag in any direction. For example to make the window wider, drag right. To make it narrower, drag left. Similarly, to make the window taller, drag down and drag up to make it shorter. If you wish to make the window taller and wider then drag diagonally down to the right. Dragging up to the left will make the window shorter and narrower.

Note that adjusting the size of a window may well alter the state of the scroll bars. For example, by making a window larger more icons can fit into the field of view. If all icons can be shown the scroll bar gadgets become ghosted as they are not needed any more. The converse is also true.

Icon Types

Icons are pictorial representations of various aspects of your Amiga. We have already seen one in the Workbench disk icon. The other icon on the standard Workbench is the Ram Disk – as you should be able to see this icon is similar to the Workbench disk icon. It is a sort of pseudo disk that uses some of the Amiga memory to store information – we will be looking at it in due course. If you double-click on the Ram Disk icon you will see that it displays its own window.

The disk icon is just one of several icon types that are used by the Amiga. There are several other types and you can get a good idea of what each of these types looks like by opening the Workbench disk window.

If you do this you will see it is rather dominated by a series of icons that look like drawers – these have names such as Utilities, System, Monitors, Expansion and so forth. Not surprisingly these type of icons are called drawer icons and they too can display their own windows. If you double-click on the drawer icon (more simply drawer) called System it will open a window displaying yet another set of icons.

The icons in the System drawer are all examples of program icons (don't try double-clicking on any of these yet). Programs are often also called Tools in Amiga parlance and they often have their own instinctive icon. For example, a wordprocessor called Wordy might have an icon which incorporates its name utilising a big W. The wordprocessor files it creates (called projects) will also often use a clone of this icon to tie it into the Wordy family. Notice this use of terminology on the

Amiga: you use Tools to create Projects or if you prefer, Projects are created on the Amiga by using Tools.

The Workbench disk also contains a special type of icon labelled Trashcan. This is in fact a drawer icon but a special type of drawer. You can use this to dispose of projects and tools that you no longer require. We'll look at this again in due course – don't try experimenting now however because anything you throw away you cannot get back. You have been warned!

There are other icon types that you will come across during your Amiga travels especially if you start designing your very own icons using the IconEdit project which is covered in a later chapter. The bottom line is that you needn't be phased if you encounter an icon type that you haven't seen before.

More on Menus

The Workbench menus provide you with the tools that you will need to carry out general run of the mill operations. Now that you hopefully have a better insight into the Amiga Workbench, have a look at the menus again and you will see that they are arranged quite logically. The headings are:

Workbench

Windows

Icons

Tools

The options listed in the Workbench menu are those that relate to operations to be undertaken at a Workbench (overall) level. Those that are grouped under the Windows heading are options that relate to and act on the current window. Finally, those listed under the Icon heading are particular to icons. The last menu is Tools and at present this contains just one option ResetWB which effectively resets the Workbench.

We will be looking at several of the options in these menus in greater depth as we progress.

Insider Guide #5: Icon types – drawers and files.

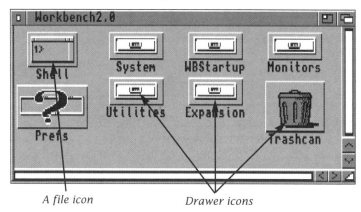

A file icon   Drawer icons

The Workbench disk window displays several types of icons. Drawer icons when opened display windows which often display more icons – they might even contain more drawers. The Trashcan is a special drawer that allows you to trash files.

When double-clicked, a file icon – such as Shell – runs a Tool which allows you to perform a function.

Insider Guide #6: Workbench menus and options.

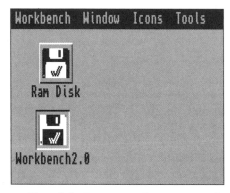

Above left: By moving the Pointer to the top of the Workbench and depressing the left mouse button the four standard Workbench menus can be revealed .

Above right: By moving the Pointer over any of the four menu headings a pop-down menu of options can be displayed. The four menus relate to the options they contain. The Window menu houses options which, when selected, operate on the current window.

Screen Drags

While windows play a big role in the organisation of your Amiga Workbench so do screens. The best way to illustrate what a screen is, is to show you one. Go to the Workbench menu and select the Backdrop option. The Workbench window disappears and the various icons it held now appear on a screen. Note that the Workbench menus are still available to you.

As you become more familiar with Amiga software you will find that some of it runs in windows and some of it runs on screens. Just as it is possible to have multiple windows stacked, it is also possible to have screens stacked.

You can reveal screens by dragging the uppermost ones down. For instance, if you have converted the Workbench window into a screen via the Backdrop option move the Pointer to the Menu Bar, press and keep depressed the left mouse button and then drag the Pointer down. The Workbench screen comes down with you to reveal a blank background (if another screen was active it would be revealed at this point). You can move a screen up and down in this way, but not side to side.

If you now release the mouse button you will find the Workbench remains in place and that you cannot move the mouse Pointer off the top beyond the Menu Bar. To move the Workbench back to its normal position, simply repeat the process. It is not generally necessary to drag the Workbench in this way, but you will wish to drag other windows in a similar fashion.

Hot Keys

You may well have already noticed that numerous items on the Workbench menus – though certainly not all – have an Amiga A symbol and letter on the extreme right of the menu. This is known as a hot-key assignment. Basically each one allows you to get to that particular command using a keypress combination rather than having to go to the menu to select it, thus saving time and effort. The down side is that you need to know what the key press is in the first place.However, as the key used is normally the first letter of the option you want, it isn't that difficult and once you have used hot-keys a few times, they become automatic.

To use a hot-key you need a little bit of manual dexterity. First press and hold down both Amiga keys. They are the keys with slanted *As* juxtaposed either side of the spacebar. Then press the hot-key you require, at which point the desired operation should be implemented and you can let go of all three keys.

For example, you can select the Backdrop option using the two Amiga keys and the B key. To do this hold down the two Amiga keys and then press the B (for Backdrop) key.

3

**Disks are as important to your A600 as is the
screen, and without that you couldn't see what
was going on! Disks are the means by which your
Amiga communicates with the outside world.**

**To realise the potential of your Amiga you must
be confident about using them.**

```
Format - DF0
    Current Information: Device 'DF0'
                         880K capacity

       New Volume Name: [Empty                    ]
         Put Trashcan: [✓]
      Fast File System: [ ]
     International Mode: [ ]

    |   Format   |   Quick Format   |   Cancel   |
```

*N*o matter what configuration Amiga you have – no matter whether you have a hard disk installed or not – the
floppy disk will be your most effective way of commu-
nicating with the outside world. Almost without fail any programs or games you might buy will be supplied on one or
more. Many Amiga magazines nowadays come with at least
one disk taped to the front. And as you become more confident
in your use of the vast array of features of the Amiga you will
want to save your own information for later use or to give to
someone else – be it a high score table from your favourite
game or the text of a book created using one of the Amiga's text
editing programs. Put bluntly, if you want to get anywhere with
your Amiga you must be able to do the following tasks:

- handle disks without damaging them

- prepare disks ready for use

- make copies of your most important disks

Thankfully these tasks are are not difficult and, once mastered, like learning to ride a bike, you never forget them. What is more, these techniques are used on computers the world over so you really are learning for the future. To work through the following examples you will need a couple of new (blank) disks handy.

Formatting

The problem with standards is that they lead to incompatibility! Whilst most computers in the world are standardising on 3.5" sized disks, the way they store information on them differs! For this reason disks are normally supplied in a blank format. So before you can use them you must perform a process called formatting. The formatting process lays down a sort of electronic map that the Amiga can use to enable it to save and retrieve your information quickly and efficiently. Because this process is so vital it is made relatively easy to perform, and whenever you purchase a box of disks it is always worth spending some time formatting them in one go. This way you'll always be able to place your hands on a disk ready to use whenever you need it. Because you must format a blank disk before you can use it, new blank disks are normally called *unformatted* disks.

To format a new disk remove the Workbench disk from the internal drive and insert a new blank disk. The Amiga will try to read the contents of the disk – it needs to do this so it knows what icon to display and what name to place under the disk icon. As the disk is unformatted it won't be able to obtain this information, so after a few moments it will display the disk icon on the Workbench with the name:

DF0:????

DF0: refers to the disk drive number. The Amiga calls its internal disk drive number 0 therefore DF0 is Disk Floppy drive 0 (or floppy disk drive 0) and ???? signifies that the Amiga cannot use the disk as it is unformatted.

Before you can format the disk you must select it. You do this by moving the Pointer over the disk icon and clicking the left mouse button once. Because we are dealing with an icon the Format option is conveniently located in the Icon menu. Display the Icon menu and you will see the *Format Disk...* pretty well down the list. Move the Pointer down over *Format Disk...* and a white selection bar will appear over the option. Let go of the mouse button to select it.

Insider Guide #7: Formatting a new disk for use.

DF0:????

Before you can use a disk it must be formatted. When a blank disk is placed in the disk drive it comes up labelled DF0:????.

Once selected choose the Format Disk option from the Icons menu.

Icons	Tools	
Open		A 0
Copy		A C
Rename...		A R
Information...		A I
Snapshot		A S
UnSnapshot		A U
Leave Out		A L
Put Away		A P
Delete...		
Format Disk...		
Empty Trash		

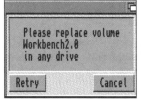

Please replace volume
Workbench2.0
in any drive

Retry   Cancel

You may then get a system request asking you to put your Workbench disk back into the floppy disk drive.

Finally you will be asked to put the disk to be formatted back into the internal disk drive.

System Request

Please insert disk
to be formatted in
drive DF0:

Continue   Cancel

System Requests

During your hopefully long usage of the Amiga, it will often wish to inform you of certain matters. Things might not be turning out as it expected or it can't find something and wants your help. To do this the Amiga uses something called a System Request box. This is rather like a miniature window which is used to display a message and there will normally be a couple of button gadgets for you to click on. Typically OK if you want to proceed or Cancel if you want to stop what it was you were going to do! Normally these messages are pretty succinct and shouldn't give you too many problems.

When you select *Format Disk...* a system request box will appear on the screen requesting you to insert the Workbench disk back into the disk drive. (If you have a hard disk fitted this actually won't happen because the formatting program is located on the hard disk which the Amiga has instant access to.) The Workbench needs to read the formatting program off the Workbench disk into memory before it can proceed. So, remove the unformatted disk and insert the Workbench disk. Within a couple of moments the System Request box will appear again, this time requesting that you insert the disk to be formatted back into drive DF0:. Do this.

Under Workbench 2.1 another window will appear and this will list the various format options available to you. For instance, as you will see later it is also possible to format PC disks, equally you can format special smart card devices that plug into the slot in the lefthand edge of the casing. For the moment though simply click on the disk device you wish to format on, namely DF0:.

Under 2.1 a second Format window is displayed on screen and you can select a number of options via this, such as the disk's name and whether you want the Trashcan to be be placed on the disk. Clicking on the Format button starts the formatting proper.

Another requester box will then appear on the screen, this time labelled Format, asking if it is OK to format the volume. The volume is simply another word for disk. This may seem silly because you have physically set about to do this! In fact this type of prompt is called a safety net because it ensures that you cannot accidentally format a disk without really wanting to – the formatting process destroys any information on the disk. To continue, move the Pointer over the Format or Continue button and click the lefthand mouse button once. Of course, if you wish to stop the process select the Cancel button.

Under Workbench 2.1 there is a Quick Format button this allows you to reformat previously Amiga formatted disks. This should not be used when a disk is being formatted for the first time or if you are reformatting after a disk has become corrupted.

If you click on the OK gadget the Amiga will set about formatting the disk. The disk icon title:

DF0:????

will be replaced by

DF0:BUSY

and the requester box will keep you informed of the formatting process by displaying Formatting and Verifying messages. Under Workbench 2.1 a sliding bar illustrating the amount of disk formatted in percentage terms is shown. Under 2.04/2.05 the display will be in a small requester type box and will typically look like this:

Formatting cyl 0, 79 to go

cyl stands for cylinder – perhaps more commonly referred to as a track. Cylinders are numbered from 0 to 79, giving 80 tracks per disk.

Insider Guide #8: The Workbench 2.1 format.

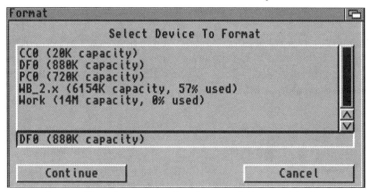

Under Workbench 2.1 a window listing all formatable devices is displayed. To format an AmigaDOS disk in the internal drive select DF0 from the scrollable list by clicking on it. The selected format is displayed in the string gadget below.

Click on Continue to proceed with the Formatting. Click on Cancel to abandon the process.

After clicking Continue a second window is displayed. At this point you can use the New Volume Name string gadget to enter the name the disk is to take. You can either specify whether you want a Trashcan or not. Other more advanced options are also available.

If you are reformatting a previously Amiga formatted disk you can select the Quick Format gadget to start formatting.

The System Request box or requester mentioned above is a common occurrence on the Workbench screen, so get used to seeing it. It is issued by the Amiga whenever it needs something from the user or needs to inform the user that something is not quite right. The message inside the requester details exactly what the problem is.

Hard Disk Users

If you already have a hard disk then the Workbench disk contents will have been transferred onto your hard disk. This means that you will not have to reference the floppy disk version of the Workbench disk itself. To format a floppy disk on a hard disk system you insert the new disk into the floppy disk drive, highlight the ???? disk icon and select *Format Disk...* from the Icon menu.

Working Disks

Disks are wonderful devices but they are also fallible devices. Consider this for a moment. What would happen if you spilt some coffee over your Workbench disk? Well for a start your disk would almost certainly be corrupted and totally unusable. Then, especially if you are using an A600, you wouldn't be able to boot your Amiga – it would be unusable until you went out and found yourself another copy of the Workbench disk. You could source the new Workbench disk from a friendly dealer but this takes time and would probably cost you a few bob. Why have all that hassle when you are quite at liberty to make a copy of the Workbench disk? You can then use this working copy for everyday use and lock the original master copy away – just in case.

Now, I make the point above about being at liberty to make a backup copy. Commodore allows you to do this, but while most companies who produce software allow you to make a working copy, it is against the law to give people pirate copies of your software.

Making a backup copy is straightforward. You will need:

- The original Workbench disk
- A blank floppy disk
- A disk label

The original master Workbench is the disk from which information will be copied and thus it is known as the source disk. The blank floppy (it does not have to be preformatted as the backup process does this) is the disk onto which files will be copied, therefore it is the destination disk. The label can be annotated and then stuck to the destination disk. *Workbench disk – working copy* is a good enough title for the label.

Next you should write protect your master source disk. To do this turn the disk so that the rear is facing you and with the tip of a nail or ball

Insider Guide #9: Backing-up a disk.

Workbench2.1

Insert the disk to be backed-up in the disk drive. Select it by clicking on it once and then choose the Copy option from the Icons menu.

The DiskCopy window will appear asking you to insert the source disk. It will read information from this and then ask you to insert the destination disk.

DiskCopy

Put SOURCE disk
(FROM disk) in drive DF0:

Continue   Cancel

You will probably need to do this disk swapping a few times until the backup is complete. Don't get the source and destination disks mixed up!

Copy_of_Workbench2.1

point pen, slide the small plastic tag in the lefthand corner of the disk up so that it reveals a square hole. Whatever happens now you cannot write information to this disk – ie you cannot accidentally format it or overwrite it. This is not essential for backing-up but it is a good habit to get into as it ensures that you should not be able to backup your blank disk onto your master disk by mistake!

The Backup

Backing-up a disk is straightforward but can be a tedious chore, especially if you are using a single drive only. This is how to back up your Workbench 2 disk.

First place the Workbench disk in the drive, select it by clicking on it once and then select the Copy option from the Icons menu. This will display a System Request box titled DiskCopy. This is the name of the program that does the backing-up. Under Workbench 2.1 this will tell you the number of disks swaps (assuming you are using a single disk drive) needed to perform the backup.

The requester will be asking you to insert the SOURCE (FROM) disk into drive DF0. In fact this should already be there so click on Continue. Information will now be read from the source disk into the Amiga's memory. When it has read as much as it can, it will ask you to replace the source (FROM) disk – the Workbench disk – with the TO (destination) disc. At this point insert the new disk into the disk drive and click on Continue. The information read from the FROM disk is now written to the TO disk. This process will repeat several times until the backup copying process is completed.

When the DiskCopy window disappears the backed-up disk icon will appear – the copy has been made and is about ready for use. Now that you have a working copy of your Workbench disk I would strongly recommend that you back-up and make working copies of the other disks that were supplied with your Amiga – the Extras disk for example. Place the original master disks in a safe place and keep the working copies handy for everyday use.

Renaming Disks

When the backed-up copy of the Workbench disk has been completed the DF0:BUSY icon is replaced by a disk icon with the name *copy of xxxx* where xxxx is the name of the disk copied, in this case Workbench 2. In other words it should read something along the lines of *Copy of Workbench2.1*.

This is a little long winded and it is somewhat neater and more convenient (as you will come to realise as you read further on) to rename this to plain old Workbench2.1. This is easy to do.

To rename a disk, first highlight the disk to be renamed (ie click on it once) and then select the Rename option from the Icons menu. A small simple window will appear on screen with the current disk name inside it. The small orange box is the cursor and this can be used to edit the name. To remove *Copy of* just press the Del key eight times until the cursor rests over the W of Workbench. Press the Return key (the large cornered arrow to the right of the main keyboard) to complete the renaming process.

Working Disk

Now that you have backed up you Workbench disk you should start to use the working copy (unless you are an A600HD user, in which case you can ignore the next bit). To do this

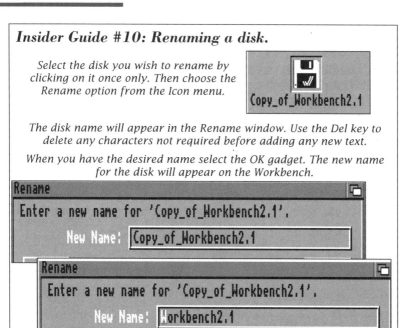

Insider Guide #10: Renaming a disk.

Select the disk you wish to rename by clicking on it once only. Then choose the Rename option from the Icon menu.

Copy_of_Workbench2.1

The disk name will appear in the Rename window. Use the Del key to delete any characters not required before adding any new text.

When you have the desired name select the OK gadget. The new name for the disk will appear on the Workbench.

Rename
Enter a new name for 'Copy_of_Workbench2.1'.
New Name: Copy_of_Workbench2.1

Rename
Enter a new name for 'Copy_of_Workbench2.1'.
New Name: Workbench2.1

OK   Cancel

insert the working copy into the internal disk drive and restart your Amiga. The easiest way to do this is to press the two Amiga keys (one either side of the keyboard) and the Ctrl (pronounced *control*) key down together. This process is called a soft-boot. For the sake of simplicity this type of keypress is referred to when written as Amiga-Amiga-Ctrl.

The KeyMap selection window will appear first of all. We are well-briefed and ready to deal with this because the theory was explained in Chapter One. When the KeyMap selection screen is displayed press the numeric key corresponding to the KeyMap you wish to install – for GB users this is key number 8 followed by the Return key. For simplicity in future we would write this as:

8

<Return>

When you have made your selection, you will be asked to insert the Extras disk into the drive (your working copy of course) and then to re-insert the Workbench disk. The KeyMap corresponding to your selection will then be copied across onto the Workbench disk. When you start your Amiga from now on, you will not be prompted for a KeyMap Selection.

Note: From this point on it will be assumed that any discussion of the Workbench disk will mean the working copy, unless specified otherwise.

Corrupted Disks

If you keep regular backups of all your disks then you should never be caught out if a disk becomes corrupted and unusable. If you back-up your important files at regular intervals then at worst you will simply need to do a bit of catching up. Of course you only need to back-up your projects as and when they have been extended, added to or contain some new but important information. And quite often it is easiest to do this simply by copying the file onto a backup disk rather than making a complete backup. Copying files is the subject of the next chapter.

However, there are a number of general rules that if adhered to should help prevent your disks becoming damaged or corrupted rendering them useless:

1.   Use good quality disks. The price of disks has fallen drastically in recent years and if you shop around you can purchase them at a very reasonable rate. However, cheapest isn't always the best and, as the saying goes, you get what you pay for. If you have friends with computers ask them where they get their disks and if they are happy. Once you have found a reliable brand stick with them!

2.   Always keep your disks in a disk box. If you get into the habit of locking your disks away in a disk box made for the purpose they are less likely to become contaminated or fall foul of coffee, dirt, dust and sticky fingers.

3.   Never, ever, touch the surface of the disk. The magnetic media where your Projects and Tools are stored is protected by a plastic shell. The disk drive has access to this via a metal slider. If you slide this back you can see the surface. It is via this that disks can become corrupted. Fingers are covered in oils that will damage the magnetic surface of the disk.

4.   Smoking is bad for your health. The smoke particles blown onto the disk surface will act as a contaminant. Give up!

Disk Space

You may be wondering how much information can be stored on a single floppy disk. Well, when a Workbench floppy disk is newly formatted it contains 880K of space free for use. The term k, or K, is shorthand for kilobytes and it is a measurement of storage. One kilobyte (1k or 1K) equates to 1024 bytes. A byte is a standard computer unit, and it may be easier to think of a byte as being equal to a single character. Thus the alphabet can be stored in 26 bytes. Therefore an 880K disk can store:

$$880*1024 \text{ characters} = 901{,}120 \text{ characters}$$

For very large storage measurements the Megabyte is used. One Megabyte (1Mb) is equal to 1,048,576 bytes or 1024K.

However, not all this space is available to you as the Amiga needs some to store its own information in. A newly formatted Workbench disk will generally have about 834K available for you to use.

If you try to copy some information that is too big to fit onto a disk, either because the item is very large or because there isn't enough room on the disk because it is full with other files, a System Request will inform you of the fact.

Talking of copying files – let's see how that happens on the Workbench!

4

Programs and data have to be stored in an orderly fashion on your disks. Copying, moving and the Trashcan are the tools at your disposal.

Learn how to drag and drop and how to use the Ram Disk to defeat the more awkward problems.

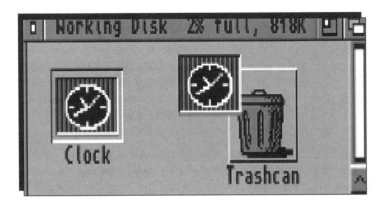

*M*oving files (Projects and Tools) from one disk to another is – despite what you may hear to the contrary – a very straightforward process. What I'll outline here is the process for a standard A600 system. A600HD users have life a smidgen easier in that files are normally copied to and from a hard disk which is on site permanently. But more on that later – for all Amiga users the ability to copy files to and from floppy disks is an important task to master.

Generally there are two types of copying you will want to do: copying a file from one position to another on the same disk and copying a file from one disk to another disk. The former is better termed a moving process because you don't actually make a copy of the file. When you transfer a file from one disk to another you make a copy of it as the original source file remains intact. We'll come back to this in due course.

The first thing to bear in mind is that there is only a single floppy drive on the A600 – therefore it should be obvious that to copy one file from a floppy disk to another will involve some disk swapping. This can become quite tedious if you are trying to copy a large file – perhaps a program – therefore it is best to use an intermediate copying stage and this is where the Ram Disk comes into play.

The Ram Disk

The Ram Disk is one of the most useful features of the Amiga and provides an added dimension of power for those of you who have a single drive Amiga because it effectively gives you a second drive, which can make the process of copying so much easier.

RAM is an acronym for Random Access Memory. This is the memory (internal section of the computer) into which your programs and applications are loaded from disk. By partitioning off an area of this memory, you can use it to save and load programs and data. The partitioned area is known as the Ram Disk and Workbench has immediate access to it as signified by the display of its icon on the Desktop.

From the outset the Ram Disk is displayed as an icon on your Workbench, and like any disk icon it can be opened by double-clicking on it to display its disk window. If you open the Ram Disk window you'll see that it's much like any other disk window.

You'll notice from the title bar that it signifies that the Ram Disk is 100% full, with 0K free and some amount of K in use. This seems weird as there are no files present – but remember that the Ram Disk is self adjusting and grows and shrinks to accommodate files deposited into it. The x amount of K in use figure displayed under Workbench is simply a working overhead.

The Ram Disk offers a number of advantages over a standard floppy disk – the biggest being speed. The Ram Disk is an electronic device and has no moving parts. Accessing a file in it is virtually instantaneous. Also, in case you were wondering, you don't have to format it like a floppy disk – it is already formatted for you.

But there is a drawback: the Ram Disk is volatile. Being a software simulation of a hardware device it is only active while the computer is switched on. The moment you remove the power or reboot, the contents are lost forever. If you wish to preserve them you must save the Ram Disk contents onto a floppy disk first. However this is generally a small price to pay for the benefits it has to offer.

Insider Guide #11: The Ram Disk.

Ram Disk

The Ram Disk has its very own icon on the Workbench desktop. To open the Ram Disk double-click on the Ram Disk icon.

The Ram Disk window is like any other Workbench window. Even though it is 100% full it will stretch to accommodate your files.

Drag Copy

The process of copying a file from one place to another is straightforward and involves three simple steps:

1. Opening the appropriate windows to display the file you wish to copy – the source or *from* file.

2. Open the appropriate windows to display the destination you wish to copy to.

3. Drag the file from 1 to 2.

Let's copy a file from the Workbench disk into the Ram Disk. We'll copy the Clock tool.

1. Open the Workbench disk window (if it is not already open) and locate the Utilities drawer. Open this by double-clicking on it.

2. Open the Ram Disk window by double-clicking on it.

At this point you may wish to reposition the windows so that the source window and destination window are juxtaposed. Note that, if you like, you can close the Workbench disk window at this point – it will not affect the Utilities drawer window which will remain displayed.

3.	Locate the Clock tool. Move the Pointer over it and depress the left mouse button. Keep the mouse button depressed and move the Pointer so that it is over the Ram Disk window. Notice that as you move the Pointer a copy of the Clock icon comes with it. With the Pointer (and Clock icon) over the Ram Disk window, release the mouse button.

Within a few seconds the Clock icon will show in the Ram Disk window. You have successfully copied your first file!

To copy a file from the Ram Disk to a new floppy disk you just repeat steps one, two and three. Thus to copy the Clock to a new floppy disk (assuming you have already formatted the new floppy disk) proceed as follows:

1.	Open the Ram Disk window (if it is not already open).

2.	Open the window for the disk to which the Clock is to be copied.

3.	Locate the Clock icon. Move the Pointer over it and depress the left mouse button. Keep the mouse button depressed and move the Pointer so that it is over the window of the destination disk and release the mouse button.

The above principle can be applied to copy any file – it is as easy as that. It is possible to copy files without the Ram Disk, but this is best done using some AmigaDOS commands which we'll look at later.

Ram Delete

You may recall from an earlier chapter that the Trashcan icon provides the means by which you delete files (we'll see how shortly). But the Ram Disk does not have a Trashcan, however there are two ways in which a file may be deleted from the Ram Disk.

The first method is simply to turn your Amiga off and then restart it. Remember that the Ram Disk is volatile and by removing the power its contents are lost. This is not very practical though. (Note: If you turn your Amiga off, wait a few seconds before turning it back on.)

The second method is to use the Delete option found in the Icons menu. Select the file you wish to delete (click on it once) and then choose the Delete option from near the bottom of the Icon menu. This

Insider Guide #12: The Drag Copy.

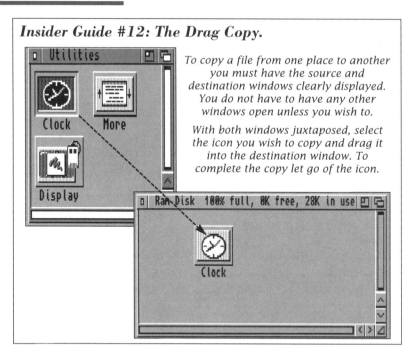

To copy a file from one place to another you must have the source and destination windows clearly displayed. You do not have to have any other windows open unless you wish to.

With both windows juxtaposed, select the icon you wish to copy and drag it into the destination window. To complete the copy let go of the icon.

Insider Guide #13: Deleting from the Ram Disk.

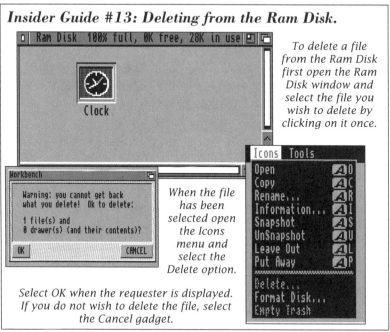

To delete a file from the Ram Disk first open the Ram Disk window and select the file you wish to delete by clicking on it once.

When the file has been selected open the Icons menu and select the Delete option.

Select OK when the requester is displayed. If you do not wish to delete the file, select the Cancel gadget.

will throw up a system requester to ensure that you wish to proceed, click on the OK gadget to go ahead or Cancel to abort the deletion.

Ram Delete

You can copy more than one file at a time. In fact there is no real limit to the number of files you can copy in any one go other than that the destination disk (the disk where the files are being copied to) has to have enough room on it to accept the files. If it doesn't then the copy will proceed until the destination disk is full – any files remaining at this point will not be copied. Logical enough.

To copy two or more files you simply select them each in turn before dragging across into the destination window. You do this by keeping the Shift key depressed as you select each file in turn. For instance, suppose you wished to copy the Clock and More tools from the Utilities drawer onto the Ram Disk, then you would proceed as follows, after first exposing both the relevant windows:

1.   Hold down a Shift (above Alt) key, either one will do.

2.   Click once on the Clock icon to select it.

3.   Click once on the More icon to select it.

4.   Move the Pointer (and copy icons) over the Ram Disk window.

5.   Release the Shift key and mouse button.

The copying process will then take place. Note that once you have selected the icons you wish to copy you can release the Shift key. So in the above numbered example, you could have let go of the Shift key at point 4.

If you have a lot of files to copy you can select them by using a technique called marqueeing. This involves creating a marquee box (which is a box made of dashed lines down each edge) by dragging it out with the Pointer around the icons you wish to select. For example to select the Clock and More icons in this way you would:

1.   Position the tip of the arrow of the Pointer in the top lefthand corner of the Utilities window, just above the Clock icon.

2.   Press and keep pressed down the left mouse button.

Insider Guide #14: Selecting files using a Marquee.

Open the window containing the files you wish to select.

If need be, position the files so that they are arranged together. Hold down the left mouse button and, using the tip of the Pointer, drag out a square to encompass all of the icons.

As you do this a dotted line marquee will appear. When the mouse button is released the files encompassed by the marquee will be selected.

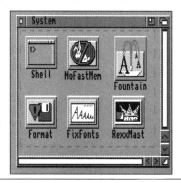

3. Move the Pointer down and to the right across the Utilities window to a position to the lower righthand corner of the More icon. As you do this a rotating dotted line will appear – this is the marquee.

4. Drag the marquee until it engulfs all the icons you wish to select (Clock and More in this case), at which point you can release the left mouse button.

5. Depress the Shift key and keep it depressed.

6. Move the Pointer over one of the selected icons and press the left mouse button and keep it depressed.

7. Release the Shift key but keep the left mouse button depressed.

8. Drag the copy icons over the destination window and release the mouse button.

And that's it. It sounds complicated but it isn't – it's one of those things that, once you have done it once or twice, becomes second nature.

Trashcan

Whenever you format a floppy disk from the Workbench it automatically creates a Trashcan on it for you. The Trashcan is where you put Projects and Tools that you wish to delete – note that simply putting them in the Trashcan does not delete them.

To see how this works take a formatted disk and copy some files onto it as outlined above. Then select one or more of the files and drop them into the Trashcan. To do this drag the file or files over the Trashcan icon and let go. The trashed icon(s) will disappear from the main window – they are in fact now in the Trashcan!

The Trashcan itself is in reality a Workbench drawer but one that has a special purpose. If you double-click on the Trashcan icon now its window will appear and you should be able to see the trashed icon(s) inside. To delete the contents of the Trashcan, first ensure it is selected and then select the Empty Trash option from the Icons menu. Note that this deletes everything inside the Trashcan and there is no safety net, ie no system requester will appear.

Because the Trashcan is a Workbench window you can see what files, if any, it contains by double-clicking on the Trashcan icon. This also means that you can recover a file from the Trashcan simply by dragging it back into the drawer from which it came (or any drawer window for that matter). However, once you have selected Empty Trash the file is gone for good and will no longer be present in the Trashcan drawer.

Insider Guide #15: Deleting files using the Trashcan.

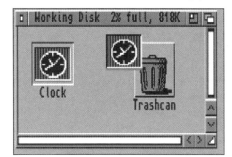

To delete a file from a disk, drag copy the file into the Trashcan.

The file is moved into the Trashcan. To remove the file from the Trashcan select the Empty Trash option from the Icons menu.

Note that there is no safety net – once Empty Trash has been selected the file cannot be recovered.

Utilities exist to help you get at various features of your Amiga A600. So don't miss out, find out how to use your utils!

Clock and Say are handy and fun utilities, in that order. Both are simple to use, so let's learn how.

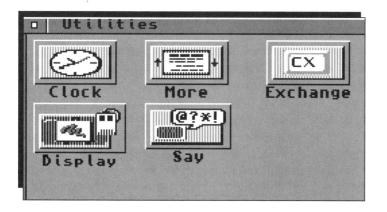

*O*K, by now you should have a pretty good idea how to operate the various basic Amiga mechanisms, namely the mouse and Pointer, windows and menus. Over the next couple of chapters we'll have a look at some of the more interesting and practical stuff possible with your Amiga, including a look at how we can use the various Tools it is supplied with. Like all aspects of the Amiga, once you have mastered one you will have gone a very long way towards mastering all the others! The subject then of this chapter is the use of the Clock and the Say utilities. (Note: For some strange reason Say was not incorporated on the Workbench2.1 disks that Commodore distributed. This may still be the case – shame.)

Essentially there are two drawers containing useful files on the Amiga that you will use more than most. These are the Utilities drawer and the Tools drawer. The latter is on the Extras disk, the former on the Workbench disk and that's the one which holds the Clock and Say tools.

The Clock

If you open the Workbench disk window (the System2.0 drawer on the A600HD) and then the Utilities drawer you will see the Clock icon staring at you. If you double-click on this icon, within a matter of seconds, an analogue clock will appear in front of you – and all being well it should even be telling you the right time. Chances are it won't – so don't worry we'll see how to set the correct time, and date for that matter, in due course.

Notice how the Clock is running in a window that features all of the aspects of all the other windows that we have dealt with bar one. If you can't tell, it's the scroll bars. They are not needed as there is nothing to scroll onto. You can make the window bigger by using the window sizer gadget. If you do this you will see that the clock adjusts to fit the size of the window. Neat!

Ensure the Clock window is the currently selected window (the Clock title/move bar will be blue if it is – if you are not sure just click the Pointer inside the Clock window at some point) and move up to the Workbench screen title bar. If you now press the right mouse button you will see that the standard Workbench menu has been replaced with a new one . Under Workbench 2.1 there are two heads and under Workbench 2.0 there are five headings all belong to the Clock and what you are now looking at is the Clock menu bar.

Not all tools have their own menu bars, some do, some don't. Just bear in mind that to get to a particular menu you must ensure that the menu of the Tool you wish to display is in the current window.

Some of the menu items can be turned on and off, in this case the currently selected mode of operation is highlighted by a tick. To see what I mean go to the Clock menu and display Project (Workbench 2.1) or Type (Workbench 2.0). As the Clock is currently being displayed in analogue mode this is ticked. Select the Digital option and watch the analogue Clock disappear, to be replaced by a digital Clock.

Notice also how the window has now changed to suit the display of the analogue Clock. I normally have the Clock running in this way but position it so it is located on top of the Workbench menu in the Workbench menu bar so it is easily visible at all times.

With the Clock in analogue mode you might like to experiment with some of the other options on the menu.

Insider Guide #16: The Clock displaying its menus.

When you double-click on the Clock icon an analogue Clock is displayed in its own window which possesses all the standard window gadgets with the exception of the scroll bars.

To display the Clock menus first select the clock by clicking on the Clock window once. Then move to the menu bar and depress the right mouse button.

Under Workbench 2.1 there are two menus – Projects and Settings. Under Workbench 2.0 there are five menus in all – these are called Type, Mode, Seconds, Date and Alarm, as shown below.

Despite the rearrangement of menus all choices are available.

Insider Guide #17: Selecting a digital Clock.

By default the Clock will be presented in analogue form. It can also be displayed in digital form. The mode currently selected is indicated by a tick next to the Project or Type option.

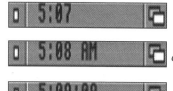

Open the Clock window by double-clicking on it – then select the Digital option from the Settings menu (WB2.1) or Type menu (WB2.0). The Clock window will transform into a digital format.

Under Workbench 2.1 the Digital clock can be displayed in four different formats illustrated left.

To return to the analogue Clock select the Analog option. The digital Clock window does not show all the features of a normal window – just the close gadget and the front/back gadget.

Alarming

The Clock has an alarm built into it. Setting the alarm is straightforward. First select Set from the Alarm menu and a small window will appear called Alarm Set. To set the hour, click the Pointer in the hour gadget box, ie over the hour counter. Use the up and down arrow gadgets to set the hour.

Repeat the procedure with the minutes gadget. Under Workbench 2.0 there is a separate AM/PM gadget to set the alarm for the appropriate half of the day. Select Use to set the Alarm. Selecting Cancel aborts the setting. Finally select Alarm On from the Alarm menu to enable the alarm. When the appropriate time arrives the screen will flash once and a high pitched noise will be produced by the speaker.

Time Setting

The Amiga A600 can be pretty much customised to suit your own particular needs as we shall see in a forthcoming chapter. These customisation choices are called Preferences and are controlled by a series of Tools that are located in a drawer on the Extras disk called Prefs. Note that under Workbench 2.0 these Prefs files are in fact on the Workbench disk. Prefs is a drawer icon even though it looks somewhat different from other drawer icons – but I warned you about that didn't I?

If you double-click on the Prefs icon is a window will open displaying the various Preference icons – again each of these dominated by a question mark. Each of these icons provides access to Preferences Editors when run. These are simply windows which provide a variety of gadgets which allow you to define and change settings.

At this point we are interested in just one particular preference editor, the one that controls the time and date setting and this is the Time Preferences editor. When you double-click on this it opens a window.

To set the current date first enter the year in the year string gadget. Click in the gadget to display the cursor, use the backspace key to delete what is there and enter the new date. The month is set using a cycle gadget – keep clicking on the cycle gadget until the correct month is displayed and then click on the date in the calendar to set the day.

The time is set using a 24-hour clock and simply by dragging the hour and minute slider bars up and down until the correct time is displayed

Insider Guide #18: Setting the Clock Alarm and Date.

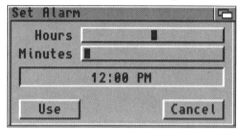

To set the Alarm, first ensure the Clock window is selected and then choose the Alarm Set option from the Alarm menu.

The two long vertical slider gadgets allow you to set the Hour and Minute for the alarm. Drag these up or down until the correct figures are shown above them. Dragging to the right sets a PM time, dragging to the left an AM time as displayed in the time window.

To display the Date in your clock window simply select the Date On option from the Date menu. In analogue mode the date will be displayed under the dial. In digital mode it will alternate with the time.

Insider Guide #19: Setting the Clock Date and Time.

The Date and Time are controlled by the Time Preferences Editor. Open the Prefs drawer on the Extras disk (Workbench disk for WB2.0). Double-click on the Time icon to display the Time Preferences window.

Enter the year by clicking in the year string gadget and editing what is already there.

Select the month by clicking on the cycle gadget until the correct month is displayed. Finally click on the number corresponding to the date.

Set the current time by dragging the two slider gadgets until the correct time shows above them.

Select Save to preserve the settings.

at their top. When you are happy that your settings are correct click on the Save button or on Cancel if you want to abort the process.

Say

If you didn't already know – your Amiga can speak! To enable it to do this then you must have some form of speakers attached. If your Amiga is connected to a TV or monitor with an in-built speaker you should be fine. If not, then you will need to purchase a small pair of speakers for the purpose – there are many available quite cheaply so check the Amiga magazines.

Not surprisingly you get your Amiga to speak via the Say tool. If you double-click on the Say icon two windows are displayed. The uppermost is called the Phoneme window and the lower active window is called the Input window.

The Phoneme window contains some instructions outlining the various options available to you. Select the Input window and type the following at the keyboard:

The A600 Insider Guide

Press Return and the Speech device will respond with the appropriate words of wisdom (ensure the volume on your monitor is turned up!).

In the Phoneme window the following gobbledygook will have appeared:

DHIY AH SIH4KS ZIY4ROW ZIY4ROW IXNSAY3DER GAY3D

These are the phonemes that the Amiga actually passes to the special speech device inside the computer's case to make the text sound more like the real thing.

Notice how the A600 has spoken letter by letter: A, six, zero, zero. If you want a number to be spoken, you must spell it out. Type:

The A six hundred insider guide

The Input window is a special window which keeps a log of all the text you type into it. If you press the up-arrow key on the keyboard you will find that the text is displayed once again, press Return to execute the speech again.

Whenever you are entering text always try to write it phonetically. Here's a short list of some words which you might like to try both ways:

Insider Guide #20: Making your Amiga Speak!

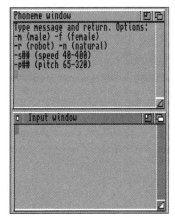

Double-click on the Say icon to display the Speech Workbench interface which consists of two windows. The Phoneme window displays the various speech options available. Click in the Input

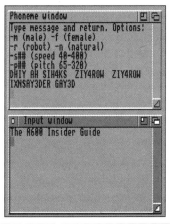

window and type in text at the keyboard. When you press Return the relevant phonemes are displayed in the top window and the Amiga speaks them!

Why	Y
You	U
Are	R
Two	2
High	Hi
Low	Lo
See	c

and you can probably think of many more yourself.

Using the parameters is easy. You just add them before the text you want them to take effect on. Try typing this in the Input window:

    -s75 -r Today is a good day

The -s75 sets the speed to 75 (fairly slow and drawn out) while the -r selects a robotic voice. For those of you old enough it might sound a little like Robert the Robot from Gerry Anderson's Fireball XL5. (Interestingly, that was the only character that the great man ever did the voice for!)

Once you have used a parameter it stays active until you reset it using another one. Thus in the above example the speed of 75 and robotic voice will stay at active until another voice setting or speed is selected. Try this:

-p65 Today is a good day

Now the pitch of the robotic voice is very much lower. I've no doubt you'll have some great fun experimenting!

To exit Say either press Return, without having entered some text into the Input window, or click the close window gadget on the Input window.

Designing Desktop

The Amiga allows you to set things just the way
you want them. This is how it should be – after all
you're the boss!

Here's a look at a few of the more visual methods
of personalising your Amiga.

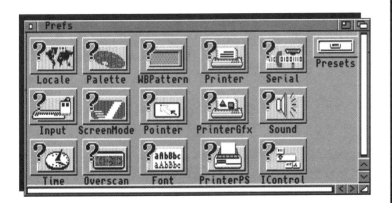

*T*he Preference editors were introduced albeit briefly in
the last chapter. To recap they are a series of windows
each of which relates to a particular aspect of the
Amigas operation. Each contains a number of gadgets which
allow you to change the way in which in which the particular
aspect of the Amiga operates.

The settings in the various Preference editors are defined by
Commodore and for most intents and purposes they are ideal
for most uses. However, individuality is a great thing and you
may feel you wish to either make your set up look different or
fine tune a particular operation of function to suit your own
special needs. And there's nothing wrong with that!

Once you have mastered how one or two operate you should
have no problems coping with the rest of them. In this chapter
I'm going to concentrate on the ones that are of particular use
either from a particular point of view or because they allow
you to personalise the look and feel of the desktop.

WBPattern

The WBPattern editor allows you to change the background on both the Workbench backdrop and all windows. This change is not just limited to the pattern displayed but also the colour used. The backdrop can be changed independently of all windows and vice versa.

When you double-click on the WBPattern icon the WBPattern Preferences window is displayed. There are two radio buttons positioned in the top lefthand corner of the window labelled Workbench and Windows. By default the Workbench button is coloured blue and this indicates that any changes you are about to make will be to the Workbench backdrop. If you wished to change the window's pattern then you just click on the Windows button gadget. Both buttons are mutually exclusive so effectively you simply toggle from one to the other.

The large rectangle to the right of these buttons which dominates the main area of the window is the magnified viewing box and this shows you a magnified view of the pattern you are using. To the right of this is a slightly smaller rectangle which holds within it the four Workbench colours – this is the colour palette. You can select any one of these colours just by clicking on it – the current colour is then displayed in the smaller box above this. This is the selected colour.

To the right of this is the Presets area – this shows eight predefined patterns. You can select from any of the patterns therein simply by clicking on one of them. Try clicking on the one in the top right containing the grey looking dots. When you do this the pattern appears in the box above the presets and in a larger form in the magnified view box.

With this selected, click on the Test button and the selected pattern will be applied to the Workbench backdrop so that you can see what it looks like. To remove this click on the Undo button and then select Test again. At this point you might like to play around with the various other patterns to see how they look. Remember you can also apply them to windows by selecting the Windows button.

If you get confused at any point remember that you can abort the whole lot at anytime by selecting the Cancel button. This will close the WBPattern Preferences window but you can then reopen it.

Workbench patterns are built up from a series of square dots – these are the picture elements and are more commonly called pixels. The

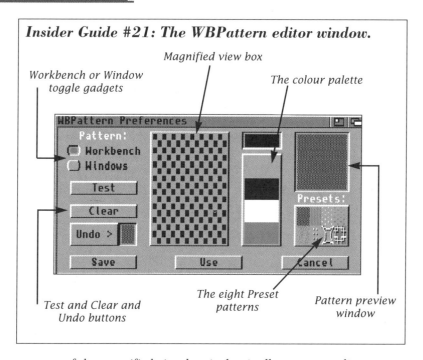

Insider Guide #21: The WBPattern editor window.

Magnified view box

Workbench or Window toggle gadgets

The colour palette

WBPattern Preferences

Pattern:
- Workbench
- Windows

Test

Clear

Undo >

Save   Use   Cancel

Presets:

Test and Clear and Undo buttons

The eight Preset patterns

Pattern preview window

purpose of the magnified view box is that it allows you to edit patterns at this pixel level. You do this by positioning the Pointer tip at the desired point and pressing the lefthand mouse button. This will set a small block in the colour of the currently selected colour. To set a blue block click on the blue rectangle so that blue is displayed at the top of the colour palette and then move the Pointer accordingly. You can apply a sweep of colour simply by holding down the lefthand mouse button and moving the Pointer. Note that as you make the changes they appear en bloc in the Preset preview area. You can make up your own colours from scratch simply by selecting a base colour – say blue – and then selecting the Clear button. You can then draw your own design using the magnified view area.

WBPattern is good fun to play with but for practical reasons you will probably find it easier to stick with the base colours. One area it would be useful in is in the colouring of individual windows. For instance setting the background of the Workbench disk window to black would make it instantly recognisable amongst a desktop of many. Unfortunately though, changing the appearance of individual windows in this manner is not possible via WBPattern.

Bottom Button

You will probably have noticed by now that the WBPattern Preferences editor has three buttons strung across the base of the window. These are titled Save, Use and Cancel and are found on all the Preference editor windows. If , after playing around with the WBPattern editor, you decide that you don't like your creation – click on cancel and everything you have done will be forgotten and the window will close at which point you can start again if you so wish.

One the other hand if you like what you have done, you can select either Save or Use. Save will record your new design on the Workbench disk and when ever you reboot your Amiga it will be used until you change it again using Save. If you only wish to use your new design for a limited period select the Use button and the changes you have implemented will be forgotten when you reboot your Amiga.

The Palette

If you have experimented with the WBpattern editor you will know that the Workbench has four base colours. These are Grey, Black, White and Blue. These four colours are made by combining Red, Green and Blue (RGB) at various saturations.

The Palette Preferences editor allows you to change the colours of the Workbench. On a standard display there are four Workbench colours and you can edit any of these, changing the amount of Red, Green and Blue in each simply by dragging one of the three colour slider gadgets left or right.

To change a particular colour first select it from the palette which runs across the top of the window and then drag the sliders in turn to get the desired effect. The process is fully interactive such that the changes are shown immediately.

The three sliders can be dragged between values of 0 to 15, 0 being 0% of the colour and 15 being 100% of the colour. Remember that the Amiga can display no less than 4096 colours so there is plenty of room for experimentation!

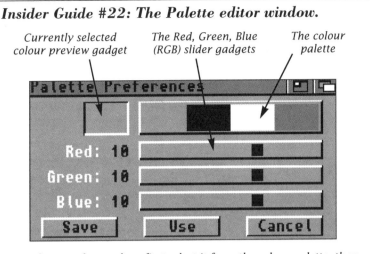

Insider Guide #22: The Palette editor window.

Currently selected colour preview gadget | The Red, Green, Blue (RGB) slider gadgets | The colour palette

To change a base colour first select it from the colour palette, then drag the appropriate slider gadgets to mix the colour you wish.

A few colour mixes are (given in RGB order): Yellow 15, 15, 0: Orange 15,7,0: Grey 8,8,8: Purple 7,0,10.

The Pointer

By now the Pointer will be a familiar object to you and because of its importance some people like to give it a bit more of a personality by changing its appearance or completely replacing it. The Pointer Preferences editor allows you to do just that. When you double click on the Pointer preferences editor it displays its own window which houses all the gadgets you will need to customise the thing!

The window is divided into four distinct regions. The main area to the right is the editing gadget and it is here where you make your additions and deletions in a magnified view box. To the upper right of this are four representations of the Pointer against each of the Workbench colours so you can see how the finished article will look against any Workbench background. To the right of this again there are four operational button gadgets and below this the colour palette and sliders.

Using the editor is very intuitive and a couple of minutes practice will make you an expert without too much trouble! You select a colour by clicking on one of the four in the palette so that it is displayed in the selected colour box to the right. Alternatively you can construct a new colour using the palette slider bars (note that you cannot change the Workbench background colour composition though). Then you move across into the magnified view box and position the tip of the Pointer at the position you wish to set a point, and then click. You build images up in this way:

1. Select colour

2. Position Pointer

3. Click

The small block you apply at the Pointer position the pixel as introduced above. To erase a pixel from the Pointer design you simply set the colour to the background colour. Position the Pointer over the pixel to be erased and click.

The four button gadgets provide a number of useful facilities and are detailed below:

Test Select this and the current Pointer takes on the image of that shown in the magnified view box. This way you can see what the Pointer looks like on screen.

Clear This erases the entire contents of the magnified view box.

Set Point

The pointer has a hot-spot. This is the single pixel point on the Pointer which is used to define what you are selecting. Normally the hot-spot is at the very tip of the Pointer and is signified by a small yellow pixel with a hole in the middle. When you select Set Point the next time you click the Pointer in the magnified view box will set the hot-spot at that point.

Reset Colour

Restores the last set of saved colours to the palette.

Editing the Pointer can be fun but if you get yourself in a pickle remember that you can always select the Cancel gadget to forget what you have done prior to starting again.

For now you might like trying to add your initials for a totally personalised Amiga Pointer!

Insider Guide #23: The Pointer editor window.

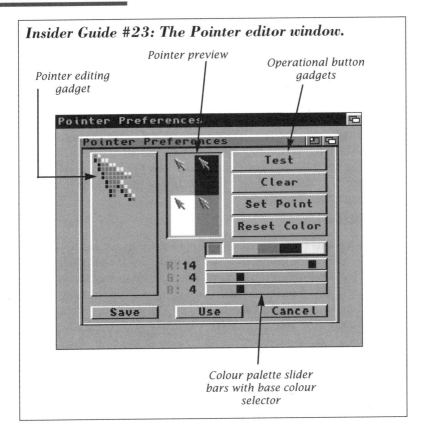

Pointer preview

Operational button gadgets

Pointer editing gadget

Colour palette slider bars with base colour selector

Preset Assets

Some of the Preferences editors allow you to save named settings which can be recalled as you want to use them. For instance using the WBPattern Preferences editor you could sit down and create a whole library of Workbench and window patterns and recall any particular one for use at whim.

If, with the WBPattern Preferences window open and selected, you move to the Workbench menu bar you will find that the Menu Bar has at least three menus which can be used in conjunction with it, they are Project, Edit and Options. Note that some editors also add their own additional menus.

These menus are there to make it easier for you to work with Presets and the best way to see these in operation is to look at a practical example using the WBPattern editor explained at the start of this chapter. For this we'll make two Workbench patterns which we'll call Dots and Arcs.

First open the WBPattern Editor and select the black dots backdrop from the Presets box (the top lefthand one). Now move to the Menu Bar and select the Save As option from the Project menu. A Save Backdrop Pattern window will appear on the screen.

You will see from the Drawer setting in this that the default storage for these is in the Presets drawer. By default the name for the file is set at WBPattern.pre. The .pre signifies that the file is a preset and it's worth keeping this. You should edit the rest of the filename though to signify what it is. The name:

WBPdots.pre

is good for that purpose. When you have done that select OK. Then exit the WBPattern Editor. If you now open the Presets drawer you should see the WBPdots.pre file present. The icon has already been assigned to this because by default the Save Icons? setting in the Options menu is selected (signified by a tick). This option toggles on and off each time you select it. If it is disabled then the file will be saved in the Presets drawer but with no icon so you will not be able to see it.

Now create the second Workbench pattern in a similar way, this time selecting the Arcs pattern from the Presets box in the WBPattern Preferences editor – this is located on the lower line third from the left. Save this using the Save As option, calling it:

WBParcs.pre

You will notice that when you display the Save Backdrop Pattern window that the previously saved definition is listed in the scrolling file window. In fact there are two listed the plain settings file plus a .info file which is the icon. Finally you may wish to save a copy of the standard default setting and call this:

WBPstandard.pre

At the conclusion of this you should have a Presets drawer with three icons in it.

To set the Workbench pattern to any you have defined simply double-click on the appropriate icon – what could be simpler! The beauty of having a standard setting there is that you can reset the desktop back to its original detail at any point simply by double-clicking on it. You can save window patterns in a similar way and there is no limit to the

Insider Guide #24: Using a Save (Backdrop) window.

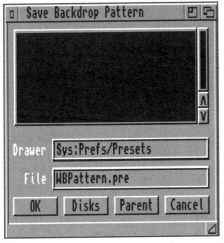

Learn to use the Save Backdrop Pattern window. Although the name may change this is a standard gadget used by the Amiga.

The top window with scroll bars allows you to navigate your way through drawers and files.

The current drawer is shown in the Drawer string gadget. This will automatically be set to Presets by this window.

The name of the file to be saved is displayed in the File string gadget.

The example names shown above are the default ones. To change either the destination drawer or file name click the Pointer in the string gadget and use the Left arrow or Del key to erase the contents before retyping.

Clicking on the Disks button gadget will display a list of disks (ie, RAM:, DF0: etc available to you. The Parent gadget when clicked will move you up a drawer. In this example to Sys:Prefs.

Insider Guide #25: Using WBPattern Presets.

Use the WBPattern Preference editor to create a variety of patterns for both Workbench and windows.

You should also create a standard default Workbench preset simply by saving the pattern the first time you open it.

The patterns are saved in the Presets drawer which is held inside the Prefs drawer in the bottom right corner.

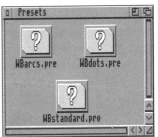

To select any pattern simply double click on the icon having first opened the Presets drawer.

Insider Guide #26: Using Palette Presets.

If you have the Palette Preferences editor running and selected you will find that the Menu bar contains an extra menu.

If you slide off the edge of this an additional menu of preset options appears (left). You can select these in the normal fashion from the menu or use the hot-key combination specified.

Note that these Presets do not appear as a file in the Presets drawer and should you save any settings as Presets they will not appear in the Presets menu.

Under WB2.0 there is an extra option on the menu – for any one who is using the Commodore A2024 monitor with their Amiga.

number you can define other than the physical limit imposed by available space on your Workbench disk.

If you want to load a previously defined definition to edit some more then you can by using the Open option from the Project menu. This displays the Load Backdrop Pattern window the contents of which will be familiar to you. Simply double-click on the named definition (ignore the ones with .info appended to them) and its details will be loaded into the WBPattern preferences editor.

The good news:

AmigaDOS is a set of powerful commands at the heart of your A600.

More good news:

You can give it a try from the Workbench. But be prepared to get hooked...

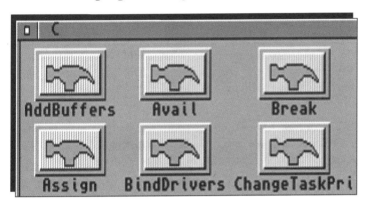

*T*his book is not only about getting inside Workbench, it is also about getting inside AmigaDOS. So in this chapter we'll take some time out for a first look at AmigaDOS. First of all, what is AmigaDOS?

AmigaDOS stands for Amiga Device Operating System. Theoretically, if you could break down the Amiga into little bundles of component parts you would find yourself with bits of hardware and software, each of which has a particular responsibility – these are called devices. For example, the Say tool introduced in an earlier chapter allows you to generate speech. The part of the Amiga responsible for this is the speech device and consists of some special microchips and some clever software. The Amiga's device operating system allows you to control many if not all, of these directly via a series of commands. A command is a word typed in at the keyboard. This is a simplistic overview but hopefully you now have the idea of what is going on.

Workbench is a *front-end* to AmigaDOS. It provides you the user with a friendly viz *user friendly* way to access the various aspects of the Amiga. For example, when you drag a file into the Ram Disk from a disk, you are graphically issuing an AmigaDOS command. In this case the command would be the COPY command.

This may all sound complex, and I suppose to a large extent it is, but let me assure you that there is a great deal of satisfaction at the end of the road once you have mastered it. Thankfully many of the AmigaDOS commands you will want to use are straightforward and their title relates directly to what you want to do. For example, if I asked you what command do you think you would use to find out what version of software you are using, what would be your guess? To find the version you use the command VERSION. To rename a file you use the RENAME command, to format a disk use the FORMAT command. Simple really.

In the above examples, I have used the command names in capital letters. This is not normally necessary but it helps distinguish AmigaDOS command names from the body text so it's a convention I'll continue to use.

Menu Execute

So how do you enter and execute an AmigaDOS command? For the odd one-off command you can use the Execute Command option in the Workbench menu. When selected, a requester window is displayed on the screen under the heading Execute a File. To the right of the heading Command you will see a text gadget and you can now use the keyboard to enter the command you wish to be executed. If you make a mistake you can use the Del key to delete it should you so wish.

Try this example. Select the Execute Command option and then type:

    VERSION

and press the Return key or select the OK gadget. The requester will disappear and will be replaced by a window entitled Output Window. Inside here will be printed the current version numbers of Kickstart and Workbench. Click on the close gadget to remove the output window. If you decide against executing the command you can abort the whole operation by clicking on the Cancel button.

Insider Guide #27: Using Execute Command.

Executing single commands from the Workbench is made easy by the inclusion of the Execute Command option in the Workbench menu.

Select this to display the Execute a File window. Enter the

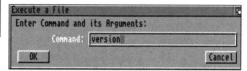

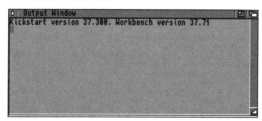

command of your choice using the gadget string.

Select OK to implement the command. Any resulting output is displayed in an Output window.

To show you how this VERSION command relates to the Workbench, go to the Workbench menu and select the About... option. This produces a window that lists the same information, albeit in a slightly different format.

You can close the Output window generated by Execute Command in the normal fashion.

The Shell

The Execute Command option is fine for the odd command, but if you are going to use AmigaDOS reasonably frequently (and you will as you become more experienced) then the Shell is a much better option. Under Workbench 2.1 you will find the Shell icon in the System drawer – prior to this it was located in the Workbench disk window along with the other drawers. If it makes it more palatable for you then think of the Shell as being a sort of continual Execute Command window!

Running or opening the Shell is performed in the normal fashion. Simply double-click on the Shell icon. The Shell window appears and displays an area into which you can type commands. On startup it displays a *prompt* in the form of:

```
Workbench2.1:>
```

To enter a command at the AmigaShell simply ensure that it is the currently selected window (by clicking the Pointer in it) and type a command at the keyboard. Try this now, type:

VERSION

and then press Return.

When we did this before, a system requester was displayed containing the version details. Because the Shell is a direct link with AmigaDOS any information to be displayed (or returned) by a command is displayed in the AmigaShell window itself.

While interesting, VERSION isn't an AmigaDOS command that you will be using regularly. The more interesting commands to the Workbench user are detailed in later chapters but we'll take a look at a few now to give you a flavour.

Dir List

When you open a window you see what it contains in the form of pictures – icons. Because the Shell, and indeed AmigaDOS, is a text based interface you are not provided with icons of the files available to you when you open a Shell. However you can obtain a list of the file names by cataloguing the disk – the listing provided is called a directory of the file or directory for short. This is done with the DIR command. Because DIR is a shortened version of DIRectory, you are producing a directory of the files on the disk! So with the Workbench disk in the internal disk drive type at the prompt:

DIR

remembering to press the Return key at the end. (The Return key should be pressed at the end of each command entry to terminate it and execute it. Take this as read from now on.) The Workbench disk will spin into life and very shortly a list will appear on the screen.

The directory produced lists two main groups of files. Those with (dir) after them are in fact drawers and you may recognise many of them. Some you will not have seen before! The files without (dir) after them are just that – files. Note how they are displayed grouped and in alphabetical order for you!

A point of possible confusion: the terms drawer and directory are interchangeable – they mean the same thing. It is tradition to use drawer when working from the Workbench and directory when working from the Shell.

Insider Guide #28: The AmigaDOS Shell.

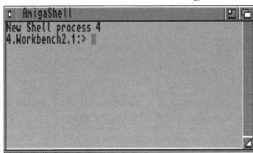

The Shell has all the standard Amiga window features.

The main window area can be thought of as a large string gadget into which you can enter AmigaDOS commands.

The AmigaShell always has a prompt. Typically this will be: 1.Workbench2.1:>

The 1. can be thought of as the Shell number (in fact it's not but allow me some license for now) and for the moment think of it as a way of identifying one AmigaShell window from another.

Workbench2.1 is the name of the disk that is the current Volume. In other words the name of the disk that the Amiga is currently logged onto. Note: if you are running the Shell from a hard disk this will probably be System2.1.

Finally the > is the terminating part of the prompt. Beyond this is a small blue character box which is the cursor and the point at which text typed at the keyboard appears on the screen.

Insider Guide #29: Entering Commands.

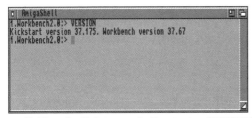

To enter an AmigaDOS command you simply type the command on the keyboard.

First though ensure that the AmigaShell window is selected by clicking the Pointer on it. Try typing VERSION and then press the Return key. The AmigaShell is also used as an output window.

If you type REVERSE and press Return you can give the AmigaShell a distinctive look.

REVERSE is not available by default in Workbench 2.1.

The list produced by DIR is too long to fit within the AmigaShell window. However, remember that the AmigaShell can be treated like any other Workbench window. You can move it and, by using the enlarge gadget at the bottom righthand corner, enlarge it. If you enlarge it to the full screen you will be able to see all the items listed by DIR.

If you wanted to see the files located in the Utilities drawer at the Workbench you would open its window, ie double-click on the Utilities drawer icon. To catalogue the contents of a particular drawer (directory) you simply specify its name after the DIR command ie:

DIR UTILITIES

Note that there is a single space between DIR and UTILITIES. Shortly a list of files will appear on the screen and many of these relate to the files you will have already seen as icons on the Desktop. You might like to try cataloguing other Workbench disk directories in a similar fashion. For instance try each of these in turn:

DIR PREFS

DIR SYSTEM

You can even catalogue the Ram Disk by using:

DIR RAM:

Extra Dirs

Let's have a go at cataloguing the files on the Extras disk (hard disk users see below). Remove the Workbench disk from the internal disk drive and insert the Extras disk into it and at the AmigaShell type:

DIR

Almost immediately you will be asked by a system requester to re-insert the Workbench disk. Do this. What happens is that you get a directory listing of the Workbench disk. This is clearly wrong and often one of the most confusing aspects of AmigaDOS.

It helps to understand what is happening at this point. Many of the AmigaDOS commands that you type at the Shell, and indeed many called by the Workbench itself, are stored on the Workbench disk. When AmigaDOS realises it needs them it loads them into its memory and executes them. Once it has finished with them it discards them. This makes them known as transient commands.

Insider Guide #30: Cataloguing a Directory.

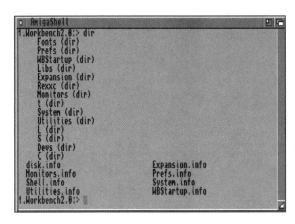

In AmigaDOS drawers are normally referred to as directories.

To display all the files in a directory the directory in question must be catalogued.

The DIR command produces a directory catalogue.

To catalogue the Workbench disk type DIR and press Return. The names with (dir) after them are other directories. Some of them should be quite familiar.

So when you typed DIR AmigaDOS looked for the Workbench disk to load in the DIR command. It knew it wasn't on the Extras disk so it asked for the Workbench disk. You swapped them back and it loaded in the DIR command. It then executed it but did so on the Workbench disk.

To catalogue a disk other than the Workbench disk you must specify it by name. Therefore to catalogue the Extras disk use:

DIR Extras2.0:

Now the DIR command will be loaded from the Workbench disk and then a system requester will appear asking you to insert the Extras2.0 disk at which point it will be catalogued. Note the use of the colon at the end of the disk name. This must always be included to inform AmigaDOS you are talking about a particular disk – this is called the volume name. If you omit it, it won't work correctly.

Hard Disk User

The problems that are outlined immediately above won't apply if you have a hard disk fitted – this is because all the command files will be located on the hard disk. However, you can catalogue a disk in the internal floppy disk drive at any time simply by typing:

DIR DF0:

You can of course use a volume name as outlined above if you so wish, in which case if the disk of the name specified isn't present it will be requested via a system requester.

8

The Amiga Shell provides you with the means to communicate with your Amiga in AmigaDOS.

It's also an open door to plenty of editing tools and the ability to use special command effects.

```
┌─┬──────────────────────────────────────────┬─┐
│▫│ AmigaShell                               │▫│
├─┴──────────────────────────────────────────┴─┤
│New Shell process 4                            │
│4.Workbench2.1:> █                             │
│                                               │
│                                               │
│                                               │
└───────────────────────────────────────────────┘
```

*A*s you might have guessed from the previous chapter, the Shell – or AmigaShell – will be the your main interface with AmigaDOS for many purposes. You will get the best performance out of your Amiga using a combination of Workbench and AmigaDOS. Therefore a good working knowledge of what the Shell has to offer is well worth having.

As a newcomer to the Shell you will make mistakes so it is worth knowing how to use the Shell's simple but effective editing facilities. The four arrow or cursor keys which sit below at the extreme bottom righthand corner of the keyboard and the backspace (left arrow) and Del situated immediately below the Help key in the top righthand corner are the most important of these. The latter two allow you to delete characters to the left or immediately under the cursor in the normal fashion.

If you have the AmigaShell open, close it and then reopen it. Now enter the following commands one after the other:

> **DIR**

LIST

DIR DIRS

These commands will generate some output to the screen. When the prompt reappears, press the up arrow key. The DIR DIRS command appears at the prompt. Press up arrow again and the LIST command appears. Press the down arrow key and DIR DIRS appears. Press Return and the command DIR DIRS is executed.

Each time you enter a line of text and complete by pressing the Return key the Shell records the fact and archives the command. This in effect gives you a complete command history and you can scroll backwards and forwards through it as you wish using the up arrow and down arrow keys.

Unless you are a pretty proficient typist then you will invariably make mistakes. The Shell provides a number of key combinations to make editing these out of your commands as simple as possible. These are normally simple dual-key combinations which operate from the current position of the cursor. Some examples are boxed below.

Command	Action
<Del>	Delete character under cursor
<Ctrl-A>	Move cursor to start of line
<Ctrl-K>	Delete from cursor to end of line
<Ctrl-U>	Delete from cursor to start of line
<Ctrl-X>	Delete whole line
<Ctrl-Z>	Move cursor to end of line

For instance, you can delete from the current cursor position to the end of the line by pressing <Ctrl-K>. The two chevrons, <>, signify that it is a single key press and the two keys involved are the Ctrl and K keys. In other words press Ctrl and K together and the text to the end of the line from the current cursor position will be deleted!

The best way to become familiar with these is simply to use them. A few minutes using each is all it takes and from that point on you will find a significant difference in your use of AmigaDOS. The only point to note is that the Del key deletes the character under the cursor. The cursor is normally placed at the end of the line, so if you wish to delete the character to its left you must first move it there using the left-arrow key.

Insider Guide #31: Editing with the Shell.

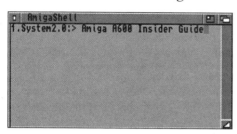

Using the Shell's editing features is straightforward.

If you have entered a command incorrectly or some text as illustrated left and wish to delete one end of the line, use

the left and right arrow cursor keys to move the cursor to the point in the line from which you wish to delete and then press <Ctrl-K> – hold down the Ctrl key, press the K key and then release both keys together.

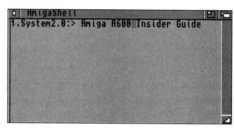

The Shell also provides a useful search facility in that it allows you to seek out the last occurrence of a particular command, thus avoiding the need to scroll through a potentially long command history list. To use this simply type the start of the command name and then press Ctrl-R. For example:

```
DIR<Ctrl-R>
```

will locate the last time the DIR command was used. Typing:

```
<Ctrl-R>
```

again will seek out the next previous occurrence and so on.

Note that this facility is case sensitive and so it is important that you use the same case convention.

Shell Commands

The Shell also has a few inbuilt commands which can be quite useful. You must bear in mind that Shell commands belong to the Shell and are not AmigaDOS commands. They would not work therefore if you typed them into the Execute Command window.

To use any of these commands simply type them at the Shell prompt and press the Return key. The most interesting of these I find is REVERSE. This reverses the colours in the AmigaShell window making it readily distinguishable from other windows and also easier on the eye. The NORMAL command restores the original colours.

Another useful Shell command is CLEAR. Entering this will clear all previous activity from the current Shell window leaving just the prompt sitting at the top of the screen as though you had just opened the Shell itself.

Special FX

The Shell allows you some editing shortcuts using special key press combinations and some more interesting visual effects on-screen using the Ctrl and ESC keys respectively. Let's take the editing keys first which are implemented via the Ctrl key – the most popular ones are listed below:

Key	Action
<Ctrl-h>	Deletes last character
<Ctrl-i>	Move cursor one tab position to right
<Ctrl-l>	Clear current Shell window
<Ctrl-x>	Delete current line

The best way to understand these is to play with them. Of them all <Ctrl-X> is by far the most useful and can save having to press the Delete key to remove an erroneous command line.

The ESC key provides for some rather more interesting effects on-screen, such as coloured text and italicised text to name but two. To see just how this works from the Shell press the following keys (after making a Shell the active window):

ESC

[

3

m

Return

The text inside the Shell, from this point, will be displayed in italics!

Note that when you press the ESC in the Shell an inverted [is displayed (inverted means displayed as a character in the background colour inside a white box). You still need to press the [after ESC though. You will also find that you get an *Unknown command error* message on-screen. This should be ignored.

When you try entering these ESC commands from a Shell nothing is displayed on screen after pressing ESC until you have pressed the Return key. Have faith!

The above key combination would normally be written as:

<ESC>3[m

as it is not necessary to keep the ESC depressed while you press the subsequent keys. To set things back to normal type:

<ESC>[0m

Some of the various ESC key commands that you can use to create a wide range of effects are listed below:

Keys	Action
<ESC>[0m	Cancel all effects
<ESC>[1m	Bold text enabled
<ESC>[3m	Italic text enabled
<ESC>[4m	Underlined text enabled
<ESC>[7m	Inverted text enabled
<ESC>[30m	Set text colour to blue
<ESC>[31m	Set text colour to white
<ESC>[32m	Set text colour to black
<ESC>[33m	Set text colour to orange
<ESC>[40m	Set background colour to blue
<ESC>[41m	Set background colour to white
<ESC>[42m	Set background colour to black
<ESC>[43m	Set background colour to orange

As always, try experimenting with the above to see how you get on and what weird or wonderful effects you can come up with. If you get into problems press <ESC>-c (the Esc key and c together) to restore the status quo!

9

When one of your floppy disks can hold thousands of pieces of individual information, how on earth are you going to know where to find the important ones?

Read on and discover how the modest A600 can take the place of a large metal filing cabinet.

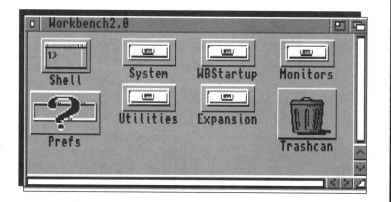

*T*his chapter is mainly a theoretical one. That said, it is a very important one because it will help you understand how drawers (directories) and files are handled and used by the Amiga.

For the purposes of this chapter we intend to look into how the concept of directories works by using the Workbench as an example. The concepts involved are all widely applicable and the graphical nature of the Workbench will help get them across. As the saying goes: "Every picture..."

With your Amiga up and running and the Workbench disk in position double-click in the Workbench disk icon. After a few moments, in which AmigaDOS is reading the contents of the disk, you will be presented with a window in which some of the contents of the disk will be displayed in the form of small pictures or icons – OK, this we have encountered before.

If you look in the Workbench disk window you will notice that several of the icons displayed are shaped like drawers. Well that's exactly what they are, software drawers into which you can place your files and information and indeed other drawers if you so wish.

We have seen that drawers also have their own windows. If you double-click the left mouse button when the Pointer is positioned over the Utilities drawer icon, a window will open displaying the contents of the drawer! You might like to try this now and see what the end result is. In fact the drawer window is very much like the disk window in that it has all the same gadgets.

Hierarchical

Why drawers? AmigaDOS supports what is called a hierarchical filing system which means that it can have multiple levels. At this point it's probably worth drawing an analogy.

Imagine your desk at home, office or school and that you have no access to files, or drawers or cupboards. You would have to keep every single book or sheet of paper on top of the desk. This would produce a cluttered area which would be difficult to work in and would raise your blood pressure when you tried to locate a particular item. In an organised working environment you would arrange your books and papers into folders or drawers which would themselves be held in a desk or filing cabinet.

Workbench drawers – and therefore AmigaDOS drawers – are designed to emulate this same process. Every AmigaDOS disk has enough space on it to hold tens of thousands of pieces of information. Most files don't come anywhere near this in size and so it is possible to store many files on a disk. For instance, a disk might contain 30 files. If these were all stored in the main disk window it would make locating a particular file troublesome and involve a fair amount of scrolling around the window. Equally you would have to have 30 very different names so each one was clearly distinguishable from any other.

Drawers can be used to organise your files. You can create a drawer, give it a name and then place the relevant files inside the drawer. For instance, you may wish to use your Amiga as a wordprocessor and as a means to hold bank statement details. You could create two drawers on a disk and label them Wordprocessing and Statements. You could then save each file you created in the relevant drawer. You might call the disk *Current Work*.

Insider Guide #32: A hierarchical filing system.

The tree-like nature of a hierarchical filing system is shown below. Each drawer or directory is represented by a named box – the first two of these, Wordprocessing and Statements, are in the root directory.

Wordprocessing has two sibling drawers (sub-directories) called Home and Club. If you are in Home you cannot go directly to Club – you must go via Wordprocessing. Wordprocessing is the parent of Club.

Club also has siblings which are Letters and Memos. Files can have similar names provided they are stored in different drawers.

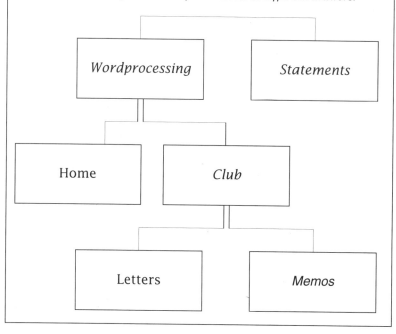

But, you can also go a step further. Drawers may themselves contain drawers. Let's take the Wordprocessing drawer a step further. You might find that you are producing several types of documents. For example, Home, Business and Club. You could create suitably named drawers inside the Wordprocessing drawer and then place the relevant files in the appropriate drawers. And we could take it a step further again. You might create two types of wordprocessor file for your Club – namely Letters and Memos. Once again these drawers could be created and used in similar fashion. In fact there is no limit to the number of drawers that can be *nested* inside drawers, subject to there being enough space on your disk to do so.

The term drawers is sometimes interchanged with the term directories, and it is quite common to refer to directories stored inside other directories as *sub-directories*. As a rule of thumb, drawers belong to Workbench, directories to AmigaDOS. Even though they mean the same thing, this allows you to clearly illustrate which one you are talking about.

The thing that should become immediately apparent from arranging your files in this way is that it makes it very easy to locate files when you next want them. If you want a Club memo file you'll know exactly where to look!

Tree Structure

Because of its arrangement it is sometimes called a *tree* or *tree directory*. You can imagine the various sub-directories being the roots of a tree, or if you turn the lot upside down, the branches of a tree. The very top of the tree structure, ie the top directory (this is the one that is displayed when you open a disk icon) is normally referred to as the *root directory* for this reason.

If you look down the root structure of the Wordprocessing directory (see Insider Guide #31) you will notice that several directories are on the same level but they are not connected directly. For instance, the directories Home, Business and Club are all sub-directories of Wordprocessing but there is no direct connection between them other than via the Wordprocessing directory. This is a very important concept and one that you should fully understand.

Imagine you are working on a file stored in the Letters directory. This is called the *current directory*. To go to the Memos directory you must first go *up* to Club (ie up the directory tree) and then *down* to Memos (ie down the directory tree).

Directory Path

When you need to reference a particular file you can do so by giving what is called its *path name*. The path name consists of the file name preceded by any directories and sub-directories which must be accessed to reach it. Each directory name is separated by a slash character. So to write the path name of a file called *Report* in the Memo directory we would use:

```
Current-Work:Wordprocessing/Club/Memos/Report
```

The last name is generally a file and not a drawer. Also it isn't always necessary for you to give the disk (volume) name in the root if the disk to be used is implied, in which case the path name becomes:

`:Wordprocessing/Club/Memos/Report`

Note the use of colon (:) which implies the root directory of the current disk. If you have more than one disk drive attached to your Amiga then you might wish to state the disk drive number and we shall cover this in due course.

The directory from which all other files and directories are accessed is often referred to as the root directory. All the directories that radiate from it are known as branches of the root directory.

Another analogy that is often used is that of parent and sibling directories. The starting directory is called the parent directory and any directories created here are child directories (or sibling directories). Obviously directories created in the child directory will become its child directories whilst it becomes their parent directory! If you are struggling to understand this terminology then simply apply your family tree to it. Your father is your parent and you are the child. You father is the child of your grandfather while your father is your grandfather's child!

10

Moving files around, individually or en masse, will become second nature but for now you can pick up all the tips you need from this chapter.

Learn how to initialise a disk, to copy a disk complete and how to work with groups of files.

```
□  AmigaShell
1.Workbench2.0:> FORMAT DRIVE DF0: NAME "MyDisk"
```

*I*n an earlier chapter we saw how to use the various Workbench options to format a floppy disk – a very important task. When you use the Format Disk option from the Workbench menu it simply invokes an AmigaDOS command called FORMAT. Let's examine how to use the FORMAT command itself directly from the Shell.

When a disk is formatted from the Workbench using the Format option you are required to supply two items of information, even if you don't know it. Firstly you must indicate the disk to be formatted by selecting it and then you supply a name for the disk. The latter is actually done for you, and a name of *Empty* is assumed – you do have the option of changing this of course.

When disks are formatted from the Shell the same two items of information are needed. The disk is identified courtesy of the device name of the drive it is placed into. The disk name can then be specified. You can use *Empty* if you wish or alternatively supply any legal disk name.

The layout of the disk formatting command is shown below. In computer terms this is normally referred to as its *syntax*.

```
FORMAT DRIVE <drive name> NAME <disk name>
```

The commands that must be typed are shown in capital letters, the text inside the angled brackets indicates that you must supply some information here. In this case it is the drive name, ie the one where the formatting is to take place, and then the disk name, ie the name to be assigned to the disk when formatting has completed.

The rules are exactly the same for formatting from the Shell as they are from the Workbench. Formatting destroys anything that may be on the disk.

To format a disk in the internal drive (drive DF0:) and call it *Empty* use the following command:

```
FORMAT DRIVE DFO: NAME "Empty"
```

Note that the name to be assigned to the disk must be enclosed within double quotes. As with all AmigaDOS commands the case of the letters for the command is irrelevant although the combination used inside the double quotes to name the disk will be used exactly.

You will then be asked for the Workbench disk and within a few seconds a message will appear inside the Shell window as follows (the CTRL-C option is not available or mentioned in Workbench 2.0):

```
Insert disk to be formatted in device DFO

Press RETURN to begin formatting or CTRL-C to
abort
```

Do this and the procedure is then much the same as described earlier. The *DF0:BUSY* icon appears on the Workbench and then formatted and verified. Unless you are working from a hard disk based system you will almost certainly need to do a little bit of disk juggling in repost to the various messages that will be echoed into the Shell window. On completion the formatted floppy disk will take its place on the Workbench as an icon.

Dual Drive

If you have access to an external floppy disk drive then you can use this to format disks should you so wish. The syntax of the command to do this is pretty much the same – in fact the

Insider Guide #33: Formatting a Disk using FORMAT.

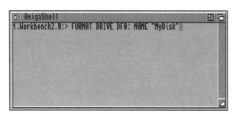

Have the disk to be formatted ready along with your Workbench disk (single drive users only).

Enter the FORMAT command into the AmigaShell window remembering to specify drive number and the name you wish to give the disk within double quotes.

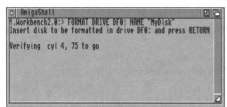

Press Return – you may be requested to insert your Workbench disk.

When asked, insert the disk to be formatted into the appropriate disk drive and press Return.

Each track of the disk will be formatted and verified. If an error is encountered the format will be aborted.

On completion the floppy disk icon, appropriately named will appear on the Workbench desktop ready for use.

only item of information to change is the drive details. Normally this would be DF1:, therefore the command becomes:

```
FORMAT DRIVE DF1: NAME "Empty"
```

Formatting will then continue as for a single drive system. If you are using a floppy disk system keep your Workbench disk in the internal disk drive so it can automatically access the programs it needs.

Copying Disks

AmigaDOS provides the command DISKCOPY to totally copy the contents of one disk to another. The net effect is the same as that described using the Workbench. The syntax of the command is:

```
DISKCOPY FROM <source> TO <dest> NAME <new name>
```

As you can see, AmigaDOS can take three different parameters and provides you with the opportunity to rename the destination disk. This last part of the command is optional and if you don't wish to rename the disk then you can use a shortened version of the command as follows:

```
DISKCOPY FROM <source> TO <destination>
```

In this case the disk is given the exact name of the one it was backed up from, ie it does not have *copy of* prefixed to it. In both forms the relevant drive device names are substituted for <source> and <destination>.

The utility works by reading each of the tracks from the source disk and writing them to the destination disk and includes the information laid down on the source disk when it was originally formatted. This means that when using DISKCOPY to backup a disk you don't have to format it first, this is effectively done as the backup takes place. An obvious time and effort saver.

Single Backup

You can backup a disk using a single disk drive. To make a backup disk with a single drive system, calling it *BACKUP* use the following syntax:

```
DISKCOPY FROM DF0: TO DF0: NAME "BACKUP"
```

Note that the name appears in double quotes. You will be invited to insert the source disk in drive DF0: and to press Return. The process of reading information, swapping disks and writing information will take place as with a Workbench based backup.

If you have two floppy disk drives you will find it even easier to backup disks. The command form is almost identical to the above process but does not require the swapping of disks. Ideally you should place the source disk in DF0: and the destination disk in DF1: and issue the correct form of the command. From the example given above this would be:

```
DISKCOPY FROM DF0: TO DF1: NAME "BACKUP"
```

Copying Files

DISKCOPY is all encompassing and makes clone copies of disks. This is ideal for that purpose but a more sedate version of a copy command, called COPY, allows individual files and directories to be copied. The syntax of the command is:

```
COPY FROM <source> TO <destination>
```

in which <source> can be a directory, file or the full path of a filename to be copied. <destination> is the information as to where the file is to be copied. Because of ambiguities arising it is very difficult to copy a file or files from one disk to another directly, using a single disk drive. If a single drive system is in use then files can be copied onto another disk via the Ram Disk.

To copy the Clock from the Utilities drawer of the Workbench disk into the Ram Disk you would use the following two command lines:

```
COPY FROM Workbench2.1:Utilities/Clock TO RAM:

COPY FROM Workbench2.1:Utilities/Clock.info TO RAM:
```

(If you are having trouble understanding exactly what is happening here – it might be worth rereading the last chapter where the directory structure of the Amiga is explained.)

Note that when you copy an icon file across, you must also copy the .info file (pronounced *dot-info*) across as well. If you open the Ram Disk window you should now see the Clock in position and ready to use.

If you wish to copy a file between two floppy disks using only the internal disk drive then you must include the disk name. For example to copy the Clock from the Workbench disk onto a disk called TIME use:

```
COPY FROM Workbench2.1:Utilities/Clock TO TIME:

COPY FROM Workbench2.1:Utilities/Clock.info TO TIME:
```

For dual drive systems things are easier as you can simply use the disk drive device names – DF0: as the source and DF1: as the destination. The command to do this is:

```
COPY "DF0:Utilities/Clock" TO "DF1:clock"
```

The disk drives will come into action and the Clock file will be copied across.

Copy files from a hard disk to a floppy disk is just as simple, providing you remember that the hard disk device name is DH0:. Thus to copy the Clock from the Utilities directory of the hard disk into the Ram Disk you would use:

```
COPY FROM DHO:Utilities/Clock TO RAM:

COPY FROM DHO:Utilities/Clock.info TO RAM:
```

Finally as you get more confident you can drop the FROM and TO out of the command line thus:

```
COPY Workbench2.1:Utilities/Clock RAM:

COPY Workbench2.1:Utilities/Clock.info RAM:
```

AmigaDOS is clever enough to know what you mean!

Make Directory

Under Workbench a new drawer is created using the New Drawer option. Under AmigaDOS a new directory is created with the command MAKEDIR (ie MAKE DIRectory). The full syntax of the command is:

```
MAKEDIR <name>
```

where <name> is the name you wish to call the directory including the disk name or, on a multi-drive system, the drive name as well. In this instance double quotes are not required. For example, to create a directory called Wordprocessing on the Ram Disk you would use the following command:

```
MAKEDIR RAM:Wordprocessing
```

Again you can use the MAKEDIR command to create a directory on any disk simply by using the disk drive name or the name of the disk. For example, to create the same directory on a disk in the internal floppy drive you would use:

```
MAKEDIR DFO:Wordprocessing
```

Note that the MAKEDIR command always places the new directories in the current directory. To change directory the command CD is used (CD=Change Directory). To move *into* the newly created Wordprocessing directory in the Ram Disk you would use the command:

```
CD RAM:Wordprocessing
```

You will now be *in* the Wordprocessing directory – as should be reflected by the prompt – and MAKEDIR commands issued now will create further directories inside the Wordprocessing directory and place them here.

Important: If you are working with a single disk drive Amiga always specify the disk name at the start of any filename to ensure the task you are performing works on the correct disk. If you do not then it is likely that the command will be performed on the Workbench disk.

Going Up Dirs

So much for moving down the directory tree, but how do we go up it towards the top or root directory? The CD command is used once again but rather than specifying a name as the parameter we use a back slash character. For example to move *up* out of the current directory (assuming it isn't already the top root directory) use:

```
CD /
```

If you wish to move up two directory levels use two back slashes:

```
CD //
```

CD can also be used to Change Disk, in other words to change from the disk in one drive to the disk in another assuming you are using a dual drive system. For instance if you are using DF0: and wish to use RAM: type:

```
CD RAM:
```

Alternatively you can change the drive or directory simply by typing its name, ie you don't have to include the CD portion. Thus to change to the Ram Disk and then back to drive DF0: use:

```
RAM:
```
```
DF0:
```

Dir Revisited

The back slash can be tagged onto the end of the DIR command as well, thus allowing you to catalogue the directories above you. For instance, if you were in the Utilities directory on the Workbench disk and typed:

```
DIR /
```

you would see a list of the files in the root directory above it.

In addition it is also possible to use full file path names in association with the DIR command should you so wish. For instance, on a dual drive system you may wish to catalogue the disk in drive DF1: which can be done using:

    DIR DF1:

Commands such as:

    DIR Workbench2.1:Prefs/Presets

and:

    DIR DF0:Utilities

are also legitimate.

You may also use DIR in a more selective manner by the use of several options tagged onto the end of the command.

For example, suppose you only want a list of all the directories held in a particular directory, you could use the DIRS option. For example to catalogue the Workbench disk so that only the directories are listed you would enter:

    DIR Workbench2.1: DIRS

Likewise you can use the FILES option to list only the files in a directory:

    DIR Workbench2.1: FILES

11

Personal computing should be about personal productivity so why not automate the actions of your A600?

Tell AmigaDOS what to do through lists of commands, called scripts, created in a text editor.

```
□ | Ed 2.00
CD DF0:
DIR DIRS
CD RAM:
```

*I*n the past few chapters we have been entering simple one or two line commands. This is fine for the occasional one-off task like formatting a disk or copying a file. However, suppose you had a task that you wanted to carry out that required 20 lines to be typed in. It could be done simply as we have seen in the past chapters. However, you leave yourself open to mistakes. If you inadvertently typed in something wrong then you might have to start all over again. No problems if it is in line one, but if the mistake is in line 19...

Equally, the lines of command that you are going to type in might form something that you are going to use over and over again. Typing them in every time would not only be prone to error but also boring and wasteful of your time.

AmigaDOS provides you with a way around this, called a script file. A script file is simply a file on disk that contains the lines of AmigaDOS that you wish to be executed – this is the script. To enter and save AmigaDOS scripts you need to use a sort of wordprocessor, in fact something called a text editor. Your

Amiga is supplied with one of these and it is called ED. In case you are wondering, in terms of functionality there is little basic difference between a text editor and a wordprocessor. A text editor is effectively a very basic wordprocessor without the thrills of special effects and other goodies such as spell checking.

EDumacation

Unlike many of the tools you have available to you on the Amiga, ED does not have an icon for you to double-click on to start it. Instead you must start it using either the Execute Command option or the Amiga Shell. The syntax of the command is:

ED <filename>

where <filename> is the name you are giving to the project file. I would suggest you use the AmigaShell to run ED until you get the hang of it. While you practice it is a good idea to save your files in the Ram Disk so make this the current directory by typing:

CD RAM:

The prompt in the Shell should change to something like:

1.Ram Disk:>

Then enter the following from the AmigaShell:

RUN ED TestED

ED will load and open a large window on screen. In the bottom left-hand corner of the screen the following message will appear:

Creating new file

This will create a file called TestED on the Ram Disk.

The window for ED is much the same as those allocated to Shell windows, however the Pointer is of little use for entering text but it does allow access to the three menus used by ED, titled Project, Movement and Edit. However, for the most part, ED is keyboard controlled and without the frills of the WIMP.

Simple Script

As your first ED lesson let us enter a simple script file. Ensure the ED window is selected and then type the following at the keyboard:

```
CD DF0:

DIR DIRS
```

ED uses Ctrl and Esc key combinations to invoke the various commands at your disposal. To save this small file to the Ram Disk and then quit ED use:

```
<ESC-X>
```

Remember this means press the ESC and X keys together. When you do this the following should appear in the bottom lefthand corner:

```
*x
```

This is the command display area and *x represents <Esc-X>. While you're using ED, it's best to think of Esc as being the command key. To execute the command you now need to press Return.

If you catalogue the Ram Disk by typing:

```
DIR RAM:
```

into the AmigaShell you will see that the file has indeed been created.

Execute It!

The command EXECUTE carries out the task of executing the contents of a script file. The format of the EXECUTE command is:

```
EXECUTE <filename>
```

Again <filename> is the name of the script file you wish to be executed. The command works very simply. It reads the first line from the file and acts on it just as if it had been typed in at the keyboard. When it has completed it, it goes back to the script file and reads the second line. This continues until there are no more lines to be read and the command then terminates.

Execute the TestED file by typing:

```
EXECUTE RAM:TestED
```

Both commands will be executed, providing you with a list of the directories stored on the disk in drive DF0:. It will also leave you set with DF0: as the currently selected drive!

AmigaDOS script files can be used to do some very clever things – in fact much of the Amiga's start-up process is carried out by such a script file!

Editing ED Files

We can now make a simple addition to the TestED batch file to ensure it returns to the Ram Disk after it has completed executing. Make the Ram Disk the current directory and then re-enter the command that was initially used to create the file TestED:

RUN ED TestED

Whenever ED is asked to create a file it looks in the current directory (or the directory specified) to see if the named file exists. If it does it opens it and displays its contents. If no file exists it creates one and signifies the fact by displaying the Creating new file message. The cursor can be moved to the end of the file with the aid of the down-arrow key, at which point the CD RAM: command can be added. The batch file should now read:

CD DFO:

DIR DIRS

CD RAM:

This can be saved with <Esc-X> and then re-executed with:

EXECUTE TestED

When executed this will switch to DF0: and catalogue the directories in the root directory of the disk before returning to the Ram Disk.

Echo, Echo...

When a batch file is executing, it is common practice for the file to display status messages to inform the user what is happening. This is what happens when you boot your Amiga when it displays various copyright and status messages as the start-up process is carried out. These can be inserted into batch files quite simply by using the ECHO command. The syntax of the command is:

ECHO "<text to be printed>"

Here are a couple of examples that can be inserted into the TestED file after the first and second commands:

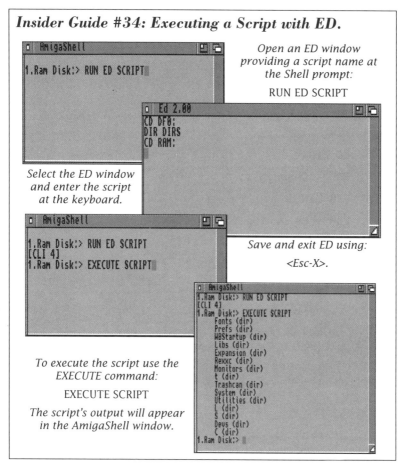

Insider Guide #34: Executing a Script with ED.

Open an ED window providing a script name at the Shell prompt:

RUN ED SCRIPT

Select the ED window and enter the script at the keyboard.

Save and exit ED using:

<Esc-X>.

To execute the script use the EXECUTE command:

EXECUTE SCRIPT

The script's output will appear in the AmigaShell window.

```
ECHO "Changed to DF0:"
ECHO "Returning to Ram Disk"
```

The new extended script should look like this:

```
CD DF0:
ECHO "Changed to DF0:"
DIR DIRS
ECHO "Returning to Ram Disk"
CD RAM:
```

By default the ECHO command prints a Return character after it has echoed the message within the double quotes to the screen. There will be occasions when you don't wish this to happen. The NOLINE option stops this Return being printed. For example, to display a message followed by the date and time:

```
ECHO "Today's date and time is: " NOLINE
DATE
```

This could be added to the end of the TestED file to finish it off looking like this:

```
CD DFO:
ECHO "Changed to DFO:"
DIR DIRS
ECHO "Returning to RAM Disk"
CD RAM:
ECHO "Today's date and time is: " NOLINE
DATE
```

Save this with <Esc-X> and re-execute.

The rest of this chapter is devoted to the use of the various ED commands. If you feel like skipping over this section for now, then this will be okay as it does not contain any information that is vital to the following chapters. It is, of course, vital if you wish to learn how to be an EDspert!

Cursor Control

Like the Shell, ED provides a number of editing facilities and these are listed with brief descriptions in the box opposite. Most of these command actions are fairly straightforward and easy to understand, however a few are worth a few words of expansion and this is given below. In all cases experiment with a simple ED file such as TestED.

TAB   ED does not contain any Tab stop positions that can be adjusted to suit your own needs. Instead it assumes a standard Tab setting of three character spaces and each time Tab is pressed it moves the cursor three positions to the right. The effect is exactly the same as having pressed the right arrow key three times in succession.

Key	Action
Backspace	Delete character to left of cursor.
Del	Delete character under cursor.
Esc	Enter extended command mode.
Return	Split line at cursor and create new line.
Tab	Move cursor to next *Tab* position (three spaces).
Arrow Up	Move cursor up one line.
Arrow Down	Move cursor down one line.
Arrow Right	Move cursor right one character.
Arrow Left	Move cursor left one position .
<Ctrl-A>	Insert new line.
<Ctrl-B>	Delete current line.
<Ctrl-D>	Scroll text down 12 lines.
<Ctrl-E>	Move to top or bottom of screen.
<Ctrl-F>	Invert case of character under cursor.
<Ctrl-H>	Backspace and delete.
<Ctrl-I>	Move cursor right to next *Tab* position.
<Ctrl-O>	Delete current word or spaces to right of cursor.
<Ctrl-R>	Move cursor to end of previous word.
<Ctrl-T>	Move cursor to start of next word.
<Ctrl-U>	Scroll text up 12 lines.
<Ctrl-V>	Rewrite screen.
<Ctrl-Y>	Delete to end of line from & including cursor position.
<Ctrl-[>	Escape character (enter extended mode).
<Ctrl-]>	Toggle cursor to end or start of line.

<Ctrl-F> This swaps the case of the character under the cursor and moves it right one position. Thus if the letter under the cursor is an e and <Ctrl-F> is pressed it will become an E.

<Ctrl-G> ED supports a number of extended commands accessed with the Esc key (see below). This repeats the last extended command.

<Ctrl-O> This command deletes the characters from and to the right of the cursor position up until the first space character. If the character under the cursor is a space it deletes all spaces to the right until the first non-space character.

Extended ED

ED supports a wealth of extended commands. These are commands which generally require more than one letter used in combination with the Esc key, or require information to be supplied with the command.

For example the command:

`<ESC-SH>`

can be used to display the file information that ED keeps on each file it creates (this is saved with the file). The above command can be entered as <Esc-S> and <Esc-H> or as <Esc-S><H>. As with all ED commands, extended commands are displayed in the bottom lefthand corner of the screen and are not executed until the Return key is pressed. Some of the more important extended commands used by ED are given in the box opposite.

As with the standard Ctrl commands, many of these command actions are fairly straightforward and easy to understand, however many are worth a few words of expansion and these are given below. In all cases experiment with a simple ED file such as TestED.

<Esc-A>
> Insert Text: This command can be used to insert text at the current cursor position. Its effect is really just like typing directly at the keyboard. For example:

`<Esc-A>/ECHO "This is an example of ESC-A"`

<ESC-BE>
> Mark Block End at Cursor: Blocks of text can be marked for various reasons. These are outlined below under the section headed ED Blocks.

<ESC-BF>
> Find String Backwards Search: Specific strings of text can be located using ED's find facility. Searches can be carried in either direction from the cursor position. This command searches backwards, ie from the cursor towards the start of the file. To search for the string Echo use:

`<ESC-BF>/Echo`

Note that by default the search is case dependent, ie the case of letters must match exactly. For instance, searching for Echo

Command	Action
A/text/	Insert text after current cursor position.
B	Move to bottom of file.
BE	Mark end of block at cursor.
BF/string/	Backwards find.
BS	Mark block start at cursor.
D	Delete current line.
DB	Delete block of marked text.
DC	Delete character under cursor.
E/x/y/	Exchange first instance of x with y.
EQ/x/y/	Exchange first instance of x with y but query first.
F/string/	Find string *string*.
I/text/	Insert text before current cursor position.
IB	Insert copy of marked block.
IF/s/	Insert file s.
LC	Make searches case dependent.
M <num>	Move to line number <num>.
N	Move to start of next line.
P	Move to start of previous line.
Q	Quit without saving text.
SA	Save text to file.
SA/filename	Save text under new name.
SB	Show block on screen.
T	Move to top of file.
WB/filename	Write block to file.
X	Exit, writing text to disk.

will not recognise echo or ECHO. The command locates the very first occurrence. Repeat command with <Ctrl-G>.

<ESC-BS>

Mark Block Start at Cursor: Blocks of text can be marked for various reasons. These are outlined below under the section headed ED Blocks.

<ESC-DB>

Delete Block: This command deletes the marked block of text. If no block is marked the error message No block marked is returned. See the section headed ED Blocks.

<ESC-E>

> Exchange Characters: This command finds the first occurrence of the specified character and replaces it with the second specified character. For example, a common mistake is to use an O in place of a zero. This can be rectified by moving the cursor to the top of the file and then proceeding as follows:
>
> `<ESC- E>/0/O/`
>
> `<Ctrl-G>`
>
> When there are no more occurrences, or if an occurrence is not found, the error message Search failed is displayed.

Note: All ED's extended commands use the slash (/) symbol to delimit characters from either the command or from each other. Slash means the same to ED as the space does to AmigaDOS so it's important you fix the distinction in your mind.

<ESC-EQ>

> Exchange Characters With Query: The above example of using <Esc-E> is fine but it will mean that each occurrence will be replaced. Of course you might have Os in your text which are vital. This command allows you to account for this. To search for occurrences of O and possibly substitute them for zeros use:
>
> `<ESC-E>/0/O/`
>
> On finding the first occurrence the following message will be displayed in the bottom lefthand corner of the ED window:
>
> **Exchange?**
>
> Pressing Y (or y) will effect the change. Pressing any other key will abort the command without any change. Pressing <Ctrl-G> will execute the command once again.

<ESC-F>

> Find Text String: This command searches forward to find the first occurrence of the string, which may consist of a word or phrase. For example:
>
> `<ESC-F>/Hello there mate/`
>
> By default the search is case dependent.

<ESC-I>

> Insert Text Before Cursor: This command works like <Esc-A>,

however the text is placed directly before the cursor as opposed to after it. For example:

`<ESC-I>/This is before the cursor/`

<ESC-IB>

Insert Copy of Marked Block: This command locates the marked block of text and inserts a copy of it at the position of the cursor. See the section headed ED Blocks below for a full explanation.

<ESC-IF>

Insert Named File: This command locates the ED file named and reads it into the body of the current text at the position of the cursor. The file being read remains unaltered. For example to load a file called Tester into the body of a current ED text file you could use:

`<ESC-IF>/Tester/`

<ESC-LC>

Distinguish Character Case: This is the default state of ED and is used to countermand the action of <Esc-UC>. After being executed, searches will be carried out and will be case dependent. Therefore the three words:

ECHO

echo

Echo

will be seen as three different words.

<ESC-M>

Move To Line Number: This command becomes very useful when dealing with long ED files as it allows you to move to specific lines. For example to move the cursor to line number 10 use:

`<ESC-M> 10`

and press Return. The line numbering starts from the top and the first line is always line number one.

<ESC-SA>

Save Text To File: This command saves the current file but without quitting ED. A filename can be included to save the text under a new filename. For example:

`<ESC-SA>/NewFile/`

`<ESC-SB>`

Show Block On Screen: When a block has been marked, issuing this command will move the start of the marked block to the top of the screen. See the section headed ED Blocks immediately below.

`<ESC-WB>`

Write Block to File: This command writes the marked block of text to the named file. For example:

`<ESC-WB>/Marked/`

The current text is unaffected as is the current ED file.

ED Blocks

ED allows sections of text to be identified by enclosing them within bounded areas. These areas are defined by the use of two markers inserted into the text using the commands <Esc-BS> and <Esc-BE>.

The text to be marked can vary from just a few characters up to a few hundred lines. The markers are not shown on screen but you can identify the start of a marked block using <Esc-SB>. Note that markers only remain until you start typing into ED, they are not affected by ED commands however.

ED markers have several uses: they allow you to move a section of text from one part of a file to another; to copy a repetitive section of text quickly and simply; to allow you to delete a section of text; and to allow you to save a marked section of text to a file. So get used to the markers, they play a very big role in effective use of ED.

Inserting a marker is easy. Move the cursor to the exact position at which you wish the marker to be placed and then press <Esc-BS> (Block Start). The marker does not occupy any space on screen and may, and generally will, occupy the same position as a character from your text. The second marker is placed in the same way but, as it is marking the Block End, use <Esc-BE>.

Blocks that are to be copied to a new position are always copied to the current position of the cursor, so always reposition this first before executing the <Esc-IB> command.

Note: Markers affect complete lines – you cannot mark sections of a line in ED as you could in larger editors. However, you don't have to move the cursor to the start of a specific line.

ED Menus

ED is complemented by a series of menus. These provide instant access to a variety of the extended commands discussed in the preceding pages. They are used in the normal fashion: select the menu option required and its function is carried out. If the option requires further user input then this is requested at the base of the window just as though you had issued the command from the keyboard. The menu options and a brief description of each is given in the box below. As always try each of these out to see how they work.

Menu	Option	Effect
Project	Open	Displays file requester to allow an ED file to be opened.
	Save	Save copy of current file.
	Save As	Displays file requester allowing current file to be saved under a new name.
	About	Lists current ED settings.
	Quit	Quit ED saving if required.
Movement	Top	Move cursor to start of file.
	Bottom	Move cursor to bottom of file.
	Find	Find string as prompted working from cursor position.
	Find Backwards	Find string working back from cursor to start of document.
Edit	Delete Line	Delete line at current cursor position – moving text below up one line.
	Query-Replace	Prompted search and replace.
	Redisplay	Rewrite current display.

All of the menu options have direct hot-key equivalents and these are listed on the menu. More detailed explanations of many of the above can be found in the preceding four pages covering the extended command set.

12

The Extras disk is the place to look for some very useful programs. Take a look inside the Tools drawer to confirm this for yourself.

And there's More. You may have used this one without even knowing about it!

*T*here are a number of interesting projects to be found on the Extras disk that we have so far avoided. They are grouped together under the heading of Tools and can be found in the Tools drawer. If you are using a hard disk system then the Tools drawer can be found in the System2.0 drawer on the desktop.

If you are using a single drive system then – to prevent disk-swappingitis occurring – you will probably find it easier to copy the projects you might want during the course of an Amiga-using session onto the Ram Disk.

In addition to looking at some of the projects in the Tools drawer (we'll look at more a bit later in the book as we reach the appropriate points) I'll also detail the use of a neat little utility called More which can be found in the Utilities drawer on the main Workbench disk.

Calculator

Traditionally everyone thinks of a computer as a great calculating device. Although in reality that is exactly what the Amiga is, the manner in which those numbers are calculated and the results are displayed determine what task your Amiga carries out. However, not to disappoint you the Tools drawer contains a Calculator icon which when double-clicked displays a non-sizeable window and provides some useful basic mathematical tools. It functions just like any other desktop or pocket calculator and you can use it by clicking on the number button gadgets with the mouse pointer.

Thus to perform 5+2= from the on-screen keypad you use the Pointer to click on the following button gadgets on the face of the calculator:

5

+

2

=

The CE key is a Clear Entry gadget and this allows you to delete/remove the last entry only. So, if you meant to calculate 5*6= and actually entered 5*7 and you noticed your error at this point you could select CE to remove the 7 and then carry on.

One key that is not on most calculators is the << and this allows individual characters to be removed from the currently typed number. Thus entering 1234567 and then selecting << would remove the 7 from the number sequence. Selecting it again would remove the 6 and so on. The +/- key toggles the sign of the number, ie changes it from a positive to negative value and vice versa.

Under Workbench 2.1 there is an additional window available to users of the Calculator called Calculator Tape. With the Calculator window selected move to the menu bar and open display the Settings menu. Select Show Calculator Tape. Now any actions you perform on the Calculator will be listed blackboard style in the Calculator Tape window.

Colour Colors

Colors allows you to alter the individual colours of Amiga screens opened from the Workbench. Its purpose should be quite familiar to you as we used a very similar application in Chapter 6 (Designing Desktop) to alter the Workbench colours.

Insider Guide #35: Using the Calculator.

There are three basic window gadgets on the calculator situated on the title bar. From left to right these are: close, zoom and back/front.

In addition to the ten base numbers there are several extra button gadgets.

CA clears all information from the calculator while CE clears only the last complete entry.

Multiplication and division are performed using the * and / gadgets.

The + - gadget changes the sign of the current entry.

The <- gadget can be used to remove the last digit of the number currently being entered.

The zoom gadget can be used to shrink the Calculator down into a small bar. This is useful because it allows you to shrink

it and then place it on the top righthand side of the Workbench menu bar for later use. To restore it to its former glory click on the zoom gadget again!

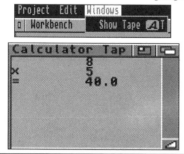

A Calculator Tape window is available under Workbench 2.1. Display this via the Windows menu.

Any calculation is now displayed in tape form. Left shows what happens when you enter 8*5= on the calculator keypad.

Across the top of the Colors window are four default colour blocks which are the basic four building blocks of standard Workbench colours. By default these are normally Grey, Black, White, and Blue. You can select any of these by clicking on them, at which point the colour gadget will be highlighted by a box. Select the colour you wish to alter and then move the colour slider gadgets to edit the colour. The process is fully interactive and as you move the sliders the appropriate colours on the screen will change. For example, select the rightmost colour (blue) and then drag the R(ed) slider across to the right. Blue represents the colour used under Workbench 2 for the window name bars. The blue in the Colors window name bar will become pink. If you click in any other window you will notice that its name bar is pink.

You can restore the default colours at any time simply by selecting the Reset button. The Cancel button ignores any changes you have made while Use implements the changes you have made, closing the Colors window.

The number displayed to the right of the G(reen) slider gadget is a hexadecimal representation of the colour weight. The three digits refer (from left to right) to the weight of the R, G and B components. The number 0 means no element of that colour, while F means 100% of the colour. These numbers cannot be edited directly so they are really only a numeric reference point for you.

As mentioned, Colors can be used to edit the colours used by any screen displayed by a program launched from the Workbench. To change a particular screen's colours proceed as follows:

1   Open the Tools window on the Workbench to display the Colors icon. It might be convenient to copy this into the RAM disk.

2   Launch the application if this is not already up and running.

3   Drag the window down the screen until the Colors icon is revealed.

4   Double-click on the Colors icon. This will be displayed on the program screen (not on the Workbench screen).

5   Edit the colours accordingly and close the Colors window.

The colours and number of them displayed by the Colors window will depend on the number actually used by the application running.

KeyShow

The concept of the key map was outlined in an earlier chapter. Basically, keyboards differ from country to country. For instance in England we have the need for a £ character whereas in the USA, Germany or Sweden they do not and it is likely to be substituted by a different, more appropriate, character. As part of the initial set up of the Workbench we installed a key map for GB. When you run

Insider Guide #36: Using KeyShow.

KeyShow provides an approximate graphical representation of your keyboard. It shows the default keys and the characters they will produce when touched.

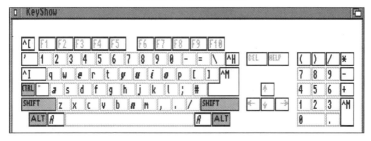

The shaded keys, when depressed or clicked, show what the keyboard will produce when these qualifier keys (or any combination of them) are pressed in conjunction with a normal key.

In the example below both the Shift and Alt keys have been pressed to show what characters the keyboard can produce when qualified in this way.

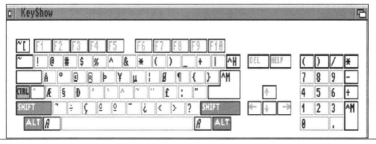

the KeyShow program it displays a graphical representation of the keyboard in a window marked with the character each key will produce when depressed. The graphic displayed does show a separate numeric keypad but since the A600 doesn't have one of these, just ignore that bit. This is a left over from some predecessors of the A600 which had numeric keypads.

Several of the keys are shaded – these are the qualifier keys, namely Ctrl, Shift and Alt. When you hold down one of these keys the result of a keypress will normally differ from what would have been produced had it not been held down. You can simulate what you will get by clicking on one of the greyed keys. For example, click on one of the grey Shift keys. The Shift keys become blue in colour to show they are in effect and the keyboard characters change accordingly. Thus a becomes A etc.

To remove the Shift qualifier simply click on it again. Press (with finger) on Alt and Ctrl to see what these do.

The KeyShow window sometimes uses a few extra characters to represent a particular action. When Ctrl is the qualifier many keyboard alpha keys are prefixed with a caret symbol (^) or a tilde (~) which indicate control characters.

More...

More is a program that you may have already used several times without knowing, especially if you have been looking at README files supplied with many third party applications. More is an ASCII text file display program which allows text files to be displayed on-screen in a window. Locate the More icon in the Utilities drawer and double-click on it. Two windows will be displayed on screen. In the background will be the More window and in the front a standard file requester window which you should be familiar with by now.

This window is asking you to input the details of the file you wish to display. There are several string gadgets to allow you to do just this.

At the top of the screen is a scrolling file list – you can use this to select a file or to display files on alternative volumes or drawers simply by locating and clicking on the correct names. For example, scroll until you locate:

S

(You should still have the Workbench disk located in the drive). Click on this. Two things will happen. The text:

:S

Should appear in the Drawer gadget and a new list of files should appear in the scrolling file window. Locate the file called:

Startup-sequence

and double-click on this. Within a couple of seconds the Text File to View window will disappear and the More window itself will come to the front displaying some text. The text you are seeing is the script that the Amiga uses to get the Workbench going, the startup process that I referred to earlier.

Insider Guide #37: Getting the most of More.

Double-clicking on More displays a file requester – use this to navigate through the hierarchy of AmigaDOS directories to locate the file you wish to display.

Once you have located the file, click on it and then click on OK. The text of the file will be displayed in the More output window.

If the file is too long to be shown in full, a message will be displayed at the bottom outlining what percentage of the file has been disclosed.

To see more text either resize the window to make it larger or press the Spacebar to display the next page of text.

When no more text is available for display the message End of File is printed.

Pressing the Spacebar again will close the More window.

```
:S/Startup-sequence
c:setpatch >NIL:
c:version >NIL:
addbuffers >NIL: df0: 15
Failat 21

Resident >NIL: C:Execute PURE ADD

makedir ram:T ram:Clipboards ram:env ram:env/sys
copy >NIL: ENVARC: ram:env all quiet noreq

assign ENV: ram:env
assign T: ram:t ;set up T: directory for scripts
assign CLIPS: ram:clipboards
assign REXX: s:

if exists sys:Monitors
    join >NIL: sys:monitors/~(#?.info) as t:mon-start
    execute t:mon-start
    delete >NIL: t:mon-start
--- More (35%) ---
```

Almost certainly the file will be too long to fit into the window and so More goes into a *paged mode* of operation. It displays the first window (page) full of text and then stops. An inverted prompt should appear at the base of the screen which will look a bit like this:

    --- More (36%) ---

This informs you that there is more text to see and that the program has so far displayed 36% of the text. To display the rest of the text press the Spacebar and continue to do so until the prompt at the base of the screen changes to:

--- End of File ---

The Text File to View window has a couple of other gadgets associated with it.

There is another string gadget based in the file requester window and this is called Pattern. By default this has the following text within it:

~(#?.info)

The tilde character (~) effectively means list all files. The brackets to the right of this are called *not* characters. The #?.info means all files, no matter what they are called provided they end with .info. Thus the Pattern string is effectively saying: list all files and directories except those ones that end in .info. The reason for this is that files ending in .info are never ever text files and therefore should not be displayed.

If the text file you wish to display has an icon associated with it you can direct More to load it directly from the Workbench. Select More, hold down and keep held down the Shift key, then double-click on the text icon.

More Command

More has a number of key commands that it recognises and which become useful when you are using it in conjunction with long text files. The more important of these are detailed briefly in the box below.

Command	Effect
Command	*Effect*
<Space bar>	Display next page of text.
<Backspace>	Display previous page of text.
<Return>	Display next line of text.
<	Display first page of text.
>	Display next page of text.
h	Display on-line help.
q	Quit.

To use these commands in More just press the keys specified. For a quick reminder of these commands at any time while using More, press the h key.

13

You may find some of the tools provided on your A600 disks are so useful that you want to run them automatically every time you turn on.

Find out how to use them and how to make them part of your setup from scratch.

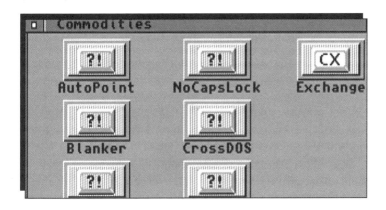

*T*here are a couple of very useful drawers on your Workbench disk, one of which contains some tools which can make your Amiga more intuitive to use and another, which contains no files, which can do a quite wonderful thing with them when it does!

The Commodities drawer is found in the Tools drawer of the Extras disk and this contains the tools that can alter the way in which your Amiga works. For example, if you have several windows on the desktop you have to physically select the one you wish to access by clicking in it. There is a tool in the Commodities drawer that does this automatically for you each time you move the Pointer over it.

The special drawer I was referring to is called WBStartup and this is in the main Workbench disk window. If you drag files into this it will run them quite automatically each time you boot your Amiga up. Therefore it is a very good place to keep your special Commodity tools – or at least the ones you like –

ready to be run at every startup. And there is nothing to stop you putting other useful tools like the Clock there either!

Let's have a look at a few of the commodity programs first of all. To see those on offer open the Commodities drawer.

AutoPoint

This is one of those tools that you'll either love or hate. Personally I love it! Basically it selects and activates the window over which the Pointer sits. There is no need for you to have to physically select the window by clicking the mouse select button.

To launch the tool double-click on the icon. Don't be fooled. This tool, like a few others in the Commodity drawer, does not open a window. It simply loads in as – in the jargon – a background task. In other words, it beavers away in the background.

You can test to see if it is working simply by opening a few windows and moving the Pointer over them. If you wish to stop AutoPoint you can do so by double-clicking on the AutoPoint icon again – it works like a switch. Alternatively you can kill the program by using the Commodities Exchange window which I'll deal with in due course.

ClickToFront

This tool – like AutoPoint – does not open a window and is run simply by double-clicking on its icon. It allows you to bring any window to the front simply by clicking the Pointer in the selected window whilst depressing the lefthand Alt key. This solves what can be an annoying problem when you have several windows open and have to sort through their depth gadgets. Used in conjunction with AutoPoint this is a very worthwhile utility.

When up and running ClickToFront can be removed by double-clicking on the ClickToFront icon.

Blanker

This is a screen blanker which turns-off the screen display if there has been no keyboard and/or mouse activity in a specified period of time.

When you double-click on the Blanker icon a small window appears on the screen. The window displays the default blanking time which is

Insider Guide #38: Using Blanker.

Save your screen by always using Blanker if you are going to be spending some time using your Amiga.

Double-click on the Blanker icon to display the default window.

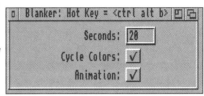

To change the default blanking period click in the Seconds string gadget and delete 60 and type the period, in seconds, you require – 180 is a good period.

Ensure the Cycle Colors and Animation gadgets are ticked to produce the display shown left when the screen blanks out.

Close the window to activate (select Hide under Workbench 2.0)

Press Ctrl-Alt-b in Workbench 2.1 to recall the Blanker window at any time.

normally 60 seconds. So if a period of 60 seconds passes without a keyboard and/or mouse button being pressed, Blanker will black out the screen. You can change the blanking period simply by changing the Seconds setting. To set a period of two minutes delete 60 and type 120. Select the Hide button to run the Commodity but remove the window.

In Workbench 2.1 there are an additional two tick gadgets which – if both checked will display a animated figure which continually changes colour when the screen is blanked out. Under Workbench 2.0 the screen will simply appear black.

The original display can be restored by pressing a key on the keyboard or the mouse. The Quit button can be used to remove the Blanker operation.

Although at first sight Blanker may appear to have no real value, in many respects it is an essential accessory if you leave your Amiga idle for more than a few minutes at a time. The idea is to prevent burn-in on the monitor. Burn-in is the etching of characters into the screen phosphor. Although this affects mainly monochrome monitors, it can affect colour monitors as well.

As it runs in the background without any real hindrance, it is worth running it, though you may find it more convenient to increase the blanking period to 180 seconds or so, by editing the 60 seconds figure in the string gadget in the window when it is displayed.

There is a hot-key associated with Blanker, which is <Shift-F1>. If Blanker is running and you press the Shift and F1 keys together its window will be displayed, allowing you to either edit the blanking time or to kill it off altogether. Note that double-clicking on the Blanker icon again will not turn the accessory off but simply bring the Blanker window to the forefront again.

The above three commodities are the ones I personally find the most useful. As such I tend to have them running all the time. So, to that end I ensure that they are firmly in place in the WBStartup drawer on the Workbench disk.

WBStartup

WBStartup stands for Workbench Startup and any files that are stored in here will be executed automatically when you turn on or reboot your machine. Normally, on a standard vanilla Workbench disk, the WBStartup folder is empty, though under Workbench 2.0 it will contain a single file, Mode_Names. This is a project which is run to inform Workbench about your monitor – you should *not* remove it.

To use the automatic startup facility you simply drag the tool or tools you want to run at startup into the WBStartup folder – in this case Commodities – as required. However the snag here is that there will probably not be enough room on the Workbench disk to accommodate them all.

If you have a hard disk system then you can simply drag them into the WBStartup folder without too many problems. On a copy of your Workbench disk you may find that you will have to rid yourself of a few of the tools that you are not using. Ensure you do this on the backup, working copy, not the master copy!

If you do not wish to do this but would like to see how WBStartup works, copy a useful tool into the drawer that is already on the Workbench disk – Clock for instance.

To see the tool or tools auto-launch, press Amiga-Amiga-Ctrl. If you wish to remove a file from the drawer that has originated from the Workbench disk, do remember to do so by copying it back to its source drawer.

Insider Guide #39: Using the WBStartup drawer.

Using the WBStartup Drawer is simplicity itself. Just drag the files you wish to run at startup into it. The WBStartup drawer always contains at least one file – this is called Mode_Names and this must not be removed.

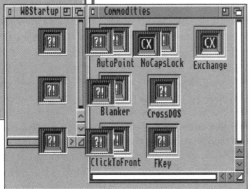

To automatically startup the three Commodities AutoPoint, Blanker and ClickToFront: First open the Commodities drawer and position it neatly by the side of the WBStartup window.

Select the three files by clicking on them once whilst keeping the Shift key pressed down. As you select the last item drag the three icons into the WBStartup window and release the mouse button.

When the transfer process is completed, restart your Amiga by pressing down the two Amiga keys and Ctrl together.

Note: Depending on your setup you may not have enough space to copy all three files onto the Workbench disk, in which case try one at a time or delete unused files from your Workbench working disk – not the master disk!

The Exchange

All Commodities can be controlled by a tool called Exchange – using this you can control each of the Commodities in use, allowing you to disable, kill or launch new ones through a simple window with standard gadgets.

The Exchange program is located in the Commodities drawer under Workbench 2.1 but in the Utilities drawer on the main Workbench disk under Workbench 2.0. Double-clicking on Exchange displays the Commodities Exchange window.

You can run and add any of the other Commodities programs simply by double-clicking on the relevant icon. They will be added to the

Exchange list and, should you open the Commodities Exchange control panel again, you will see them listed.

We'll come back to the use of the Commodities Exchange program when we have had a look at what the Commodities programs supplied on the Extras disk do. These are located in the Commodities drawer which is to be found inside the Tools drawer.

The Exchange control program window may well be self-explanatory to you at this stage. Certainly it is no more complex than any other Workbench orientated window we have encountered to date.

Each commodity that is running is listed in the Available Commodities window which is positioned roughly centrally in the Exchange window itself. If none are listed then none are running.

You can select any commodity in the Available Commodities window simply by clicking on it once. When you do this the three text gadget lines below the window marked Title, Description, Status will be filled with information relating to the selected commodity. The first two of these are self-explanatory. The Status position will be filled with one of two conditions, namely Enabled or Disabled.

When a commodity is run it will be enabled and therefore be fully functional. It can be disabled by clicking on the Disable gadget on the righthand window. This is useful when you want to stop the functionality of the commodity but anticipate needing to use it again shortly, in which case you can select it in the Available Commodities window and select the Enable gadget. To remove a commodity totally you select the commodity in the Available Commodities window and then select the Kill gadget.

The Show gadget brings the window for the selected commodity to the front of the screen. If the window is closed Show opens it. This gadget is only applicable therefore to the commodities that have windows available to them, namely Blanker, and FKey. Once displayed the window can be hidden by selecting the Hide gadget (on the left of Show).

The remaining two gadget buttons, Hide and Quit on the left of the Exchange window, affect Exchange itself. Hide removes the Exchange window from the screen – it can be recalled again by pressing <Alt-Help>. Quit removes the Exchange program from memory, however any resident commodities already in use will still be available. The net effect of Quit is that you cannot hot-key the Exchange window into life with the <Alt-Help> combination, you have to run the Exchange pro-

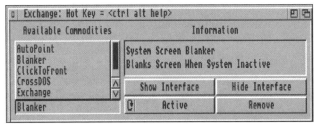

Insider Guide #40: Using Commodity Exchange.

The Exchange window allows you control over all active commodities whether they open a window or not. All currently loaded commodities are listed in a scrolling window. Click on any name in the window once to select it. Information regarding its function is displayed.

After selection a commodity can be made active or inactive and may also be removed from memory.

Selecting Remove (Kill on Workbench 2.0) will remove the commodity completely.

When the Exchange window is hidden it can be redisplayed by pressing the Ctrl, Alt and Help keys down together.

gram by double-clicking on its icon in the Utilities Drawer of the Workbench disk.

FKey Control

FKey allows you to assign a string of characters to a specific function key. It is intended to make repetitive tasks, like entering AmigaDOS commands, easier by assigning them to function keys. Although essentially the same in operation the commodity provides much greater functionality in Workbench 2.1 – it also looks rather different. Let's concentrate on FKey under Workbench 2.1 first.

When you double-click on the FKey icon its window is displayed. You can assign strings to every function key and shifted function key (that is the same function key pressed in combination with the Shift key), thus providing up to 20 functions for definition.

There is a cycle gadget which allows you to select from a series of functions available from the function keys, these include Run program and Insert Text. For instance you could run your favourite program directly simply by pressing a function key. For example, to run DPAINT or a similar program by pressing Alt-F1 you would take the four simple steps:

*   Click on New Key gadget

- Enter the following into the string gadget:

  alt f1

- Select the Run Program option from the Cycle cycle gadget.

- Enter the name (including path if any) of the program into the Command Parameters string gadget, ie:

  DPAINT

This and any further definitions can be saved using the Save Define Keys option from FKeys Project menu. When Alt-F1 is pressed the function defined is carried out.

For Workbench 2.0 FKey is provided with a number of predefined functions which are listed as strings in a series of small string gadget windows. Each of these is terminated by \n and this is interpreted as Return and has the same effect as pressing the Return key. Notice that each function key definition is terminated by this character combination. If it is missed off then you will have to physically press the Return key after selecting the desired function key to implement the command.

By default, under Workbench 2.0 function keys F1, F2 and F3 are defined as follows:

F1	Status Full	Provide full Status listing
F2	Dir	Catalogue current directory
F3	List	List all files

New strings can be added simply by clicking the Pointer in the required text gadget and typing in your text. For example to assign the AmigaDOS command to catalogue the Ram Disk to function key F9, proceed as follows:

1. Display the FKey window.

2. Click in the text gadget next to F9.

3. Type:

   DIR RAM:\n

When you have entered your desired strings, select the Use button to implement them and then the Hide gadget to remove the FKey window. To use a key to issue an AmigaDOS command, first either select Execute Command from the Workbench menu or open an AmigaDOS Shell. Then press the desired function key. If the command is assigned

Insider Guide #41: Using FKey under Workbench 2.1

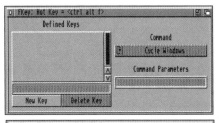

The FKey window has a number of simple but effective gadgets that allow access to a wide range of user-definable features at the press of a function key.

Programs – including AmigaDOS commands can be made available.

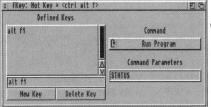

Click on New Key and enter the text alt f1 into the string gadget. Click on the Command cycle gadget until RUN Program is displayed. Enter STATUS in the Command Parameters string gadget.

Text strings can be assigned to keys in the same way, simply cycle through the Command gadget until Insert Text is displayed.

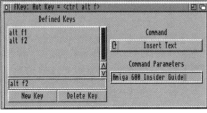

Save by closing the window.

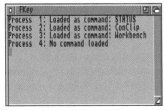

To use the STATUS command simply hold down the Alt key and press F1 before releasing both keys.

The STATUS command will be run and its output displayed in its own FKey window.

to a shifted function key remember to hold down the Shift key as you press the required function key.

You are not limited to using AmigaDOS commands, you can assign any text you require to the keys. Thus, if you are using ED or similar and have trouble spelling certain words, you could assign each to a function key and simply select the required function key at each point. In such a circumstance there would be no need for you to include the \n Return character at the end of each line.

The FKey strings that you enter into the text gadgets are not, by default, saved. Thus when you turn off or reboot your Amiga any FKey settings will be lost.

NoCapsLock

This Commodity does not open a window. When run it effectively disables the Caps Lock key on the keyboard. Other keys such as the Shift key remain functional. When pressed and turned on Caps Lock forces all keystrokes to capital letters, thus if an a is typed, A will be produced.

With NoCapsLock in force capital letters can still be produced, by holding the Shift key down when pressing the appropriate letter on the keyboard.

NoCapsLock can be disabled or killed from the Exchange window or by running it again, ie by double-clicking on its icon.

Icons make the Amiga both distinctive and intuitive to use.

Learn how to edit and design your very own to add that personal touch, using the Amiga's very own software to do the job!

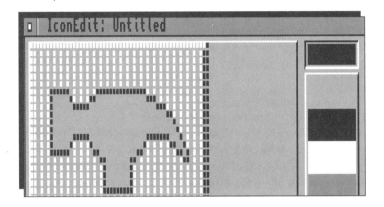

One of the features that makes the Amiga unique, is its icons. They are distinctive and intuitive to use. They have a look which tries to approximate the type of tool or project they are associated with. There are five basic icon types – although you may not have seen all of these to date.

You may recall from an earlier chapter that icons are not stored as part of the original program or file they create. They are stored as .info (dot-info) files. For instance the icon associated with the Shell is in fact called:

Shell.info

You can see these and other .info files simply by opening a Shell window and typing:

DIR

to list all the files, picking out the ones with the .info postfix. These hold the graphic information which displays the picture on screen and also the information or pointer linking them to a particular file.

If you examine the listing in relation to the Workbench disk window itself you will see that there is a .info file for each of the icons that are displayed.

Icon Types

What might not be apparent at this point is that there are several basic icon types although the typical on-screen appearance of the icon may change. These basic icon types are:

Disk

Drawer

Tool

Project

Trashcan

A Disk icon represents any disk that is available or accessible by the Workbench. The Ram Disk and Workbench disk icons are the standard format though, as you may have already noticed from third-party applications, icons can be vastly different and may even be very much larger! When you open a disk icon, a window will always appear on the screen displaying any icon files that are available in the disk's root directory.

A Drawer icon represents a subdivision of the disk's storage area. When a drawer icon is opened a window will appear displaying any icon files that are held within the drawer's directory. The System drawer is a typical drawer icon, however the Prefs icon is also a drawer icon!

A Tool icon represents a program. The appearance of these is normally unique. When you open a tool icon you start the program it is linked to. The Clock and Calculator icons are examples of Tool icons.

A Project icon represents a file that has been created by a tool, ie a program. Again it may be very specific in appearance but as a general rule it will look similar to the tool icon from which it was created. When you open a Project icon it will normally first load the tool which created it and then the file associated with the project.

The Trashcan icon represents an area on the disk where unwanted items are stored until you decide to discard them by emptying the trash!

Insider Guide #42: Icon types and operation.

There are five basic icon types although icons of the same type do not always look the same. That said, icons of the same type always carry out the same action when double-clicked.

The Disk icon – as used for the Workbench disk – will display a window showing the files and drawers it contains.

A Drawer icon normally – though not always – takes the shape of a drawer. When it is opened it will display a window showing any icons it may contain.

A Tool icon can take many guises. However, when double-clicked, it will normally run a program – a tool – that can be used to perform a job. The Clock and Calculator are examples of tools.

A Project icon is generated by a tool. For example, a text file generated by a wordprocessor. The Project icon will often look similar to the Tool icon that created it. When the Project icon is double-clicked it will normally load the tool that created it and load the information in the project into the tool.

The Trashcan icon is unique – as is the Trashcan which is itself a drawer. Like any other drawer it may be opened to display a window.

Creating Icons

Supplied on your Amiga Workbench disk is the means to enable you to create, edit and even personalise your own icons, either starting from existing icons or from scratch for new projects you are yourself creating. With just a little imagination you could transform your Workbench to make it look like nobody else's.

The key to achieving this is IconEdit, which can be found in the Tools directory on the Extras disk.

Icon Editing

When you double-click on the IconEdit icon it reveals its own window along with a full set of menus. By default the IconEdit window contains a magnified version of an icon, a hammerhead, in the drawing area, a colour menu to its right and a toolbox of drawing tools. The extreme right of the window also contains an actual size image of the current icon – you may already have noticed this.

From this point you can create your own icon using the hammerhead as a base to work from or, alternatively edit an existing icon by loading it into IconEdit, or perhaps clear the field to start from scratch.

If you wish to create your own icon from scratch locate the Clear gadget at the bottom of the drawing tools and click to clear the drawing area to a grid pattern. This is useful for guiding your drawing tools especially since icons are usually pretty structured designs. However, it can be turned off via the Settings menu.

Each of the grid squares represent a pixel and these can be set in any of the four Workbench colours – the desired colour being selected from the colour menu. You can clear the background to a particular colour simply by selecting the colour required and then clicking on Clear. You can then select a desired colour and click the left mouse button within the drawing area to set points and thereby build up your design. The point to be set should be positioned centrally within the cross-hair cursor. To aid you further the coordinates of the cross-hair cursor are displayed in the window title bar and run from 1,1 in the top lefthand corner to 80,0 in the bottom right. Therefore the desired area is 80 pixels wide and 40 deep.

One important gadget to be aware of at the off is the Undo button. Pressing this will undo your last action – but only the last one.

The toolbox below the colour menu provides six simple but effective drawing tools which are easily learnt by a bit of experimentation. The tools are:

Freehand   This is a sort of perpetual draw tool and while you keep the mouse button down it will draw a continuous line of pixels in the currently selected colour as you move the mouse over the drawing area.

Continuous Freehand
               This gadget is similar to the Freehand gadget described above except that it will always produce a

Insider Guide #42: Using IconEdit.

The Magnified View Area: Drawing actions are performed here by positioning the tip of the point and clicking. The point is then set in the selected colour – points can be erased by using the background colour.

The Actual Size Preview Area: Your icon design is displayed actual size in this area – in this way you can see how it will look on-screen.

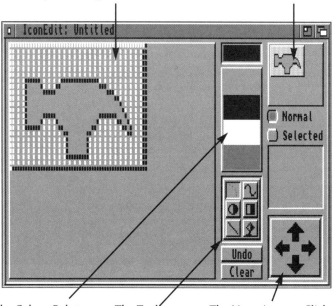

The Colour Palette: Click on any colour to select it. The selected colour is displayed at the top.

The Toolbox: Six basic tools are provided for your use.

The Move Arrows: Click on the arrow heads to position your icon design. Use with care – scrolling an icon or part of it off the magnified view area erases it.

continuous line. That said, to create the continuous line you must move more sedately than you might for the aforementioned Freehand gadget.

Circle   This gadget allows you to draw a circle in the selected colour. To draw a a circle click at the point in the drawing area where you wish the centre of the circle to be. Then drag the Pointer away from the point to create the circle size you wish. You can move the Pointer to and fro from the centre to alter the size of the circle. You can even extend the circle off screen. Once you release the mouse button the circle will be set. Note that the icon of the gadget has a filled half. If you select this you will get a circle that is filled in the selected colour. If you select the unfilled segment you will get only the circle outline. In the case of the latter, if you draw the circle and then press the Ctrl key before releasing the mouse button the thickness of the circle outline will be doubled!

Box   The box gadget works in much the same way as Circle to create rectangles except that the initial mouse click sets the top left corner of the square and you then drag down and across to the desired bottom righthand corner. In addition to doubling the line thickness as indicated above you can also create a 3D box effect (similar to that shown around Workbench icons) by holding down the Alt key before releasing the mouse button.

Line   Not surprisingly this allows you to draw a line at any angle. Simply click at the start point and drag the Pointer to the desired end point. If you press Ctrl before releasing the mouse button the line thickness will be doubled.

Fill   The fill gadget allows you to fill an enclosed area with a selected colour. For example you could draw a rectangle in black on a white background and then in-fill it with blue. To do this simply select the fill colour, the fill gadget and move the Pointer inside the enclosed area before clicking the left mouse button.

IconEdit Menus

IconEdit provides you with a total of seven menus which provide between them a host of useful features. The function of many of these should be reasonably clear to you as we have encountered options with similar actions before. Some of the more erudite functions are explained below.

The Project menu is a standard interface that allows you to open and save icon files for editing or creation. The Save As Default option allows you to design your own default tools and save them. For example, the default tool icon is the hammerhead icon – you could change this by using the Type menu to select the desired default tool and then

Insider Guide #44: The IconEdit Toolbox.

Freehand Gadget

Continuous Freehand Gadget

Circle Gadget

Box Gadget

Line Gadget

Fill Gadget

edit it. . For instance the default disk icon – as used by the Ram Disk etc – has no colour. You could change the black tick into a blue one as follows:

1. Select Disk from the Type menu.

2. Select New from the Project menu.

3. Select the blue colour from the colour gadget.

4. Click on each black pixel comprising the tick to make it blue.

5. Select the Save As Default Icon option from the Project menu. (The default information is saved to our Workbench disk.)

6. Insert a new disk into a disk drive.

If you have proceeded correctly the icon representing the new disk – and all subsequent disk icons – should now have a blue tick!

The Edit Menu introduces the concept of the clipboard. In reality this is simply an area of Amiga memory into which images can be held temporarily. Like the Ram Disk it is volatile so its contents are lost when you close IconEdit or reboot. Note also that only one image can be held in the clipboard, so loading a second will cause the original or previous image to be overwritten.

The Highlights menu includes the Image option that can be used to create a second icon to be shown when the original is displayed (this is explained shortly). It also includes two other interesting options Complement and Backfill. If you select Complement when designing an icon (with the Normal radio button checked) then when you select the icon it will be highlighted, including the background of the box. You can see the physical effect of this by clicking once on the Ram Disk icon for instance. The Backfill option works in much the same fashion except that the background box is not highlighted.

A word of warning. Those big black arrows in the corner of the IconEdit window can erase your work if you are not careful. While they are great for getting an icon in the right position on-screen, if any part of the icon goes off-screen it will be lost. Take care in using them and don't scroll too fast.

Double Identity

You may have noticed two other button gadgets in the IconEdit window – Normal and Selected. As a matter of course you will normally work with the Normal button selected.

If you have used third party applications or opened an icon from a magazine then you will have probably noticed that when you selected the icon it changed to a new icon. In other words there was an image for the unselected icon and a different image for the selected icon. This is quite easy to achieve and essentially just involves you creating a second icon image to go with the first. To do this you will first need to create the first – normal – icon. With this loaded you will need to select the image option from the Highlight menu (part of the IconEdit suite of menus in the menu bar). Then you can click the Selected radio button which will then allow you to create a new, ie second icon. Once completed you can save this using Save from the project menu. Now when you click on your icon design it will take on its new selected form.

Icon Affairs

Creating simple but effective icons is quite an art and it may take you a good deal of practice to produce designs you find really appealing. For the most part, if you should concentrate on editing existing icons so that your Workbench becomes a more personal affair.

Remember though to only edit those on the working copy of your Workbench disk.

Remember also that icons should be recognisable for what they represent and you may have noticed the real-size picture which is displayed

Insider Guide #45: Creating an Icon from scratch.

Open IconEdit, select Black as a colour (by clicking on the black box in the colour palette) and then click on the Clear gadget to set the drawing area to black. Then select white as the current colour.

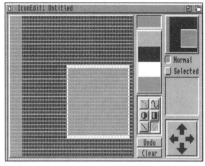

Select the outline Box gadget and drag out a simple rectangle roughly central in the screen – I used coordinates 30,15 to 70,35. Select blue as the current colour.

Select the Fill gadget and move the Pointer inside the newly drawn rectangle before pressing the lefthand mouse button. This will fill in the rectangle with blue.

Locate the four large arrows at the bottom righthand corner of the window and press on the one pointing right about 6-8 times to nudge the screen to the right. The arrows can be used to enable you to accurately position a design, for instance in the centre of the screen or at the top left – as you wish. However, in doing so it has created a band of grey down the lefthand side of the icon. This can be left if you wish or alternatively you can set it to black or another colour.

For example: Select blue as the current colour. Select the Fill gadget and click in the uncoloured area.

The final image on screen should look something like that shown. The next step is to name and save the icon.

From the Project menu select the Save option to display a standard Workbench file requester. Select the Disks gadget and then RAM:.

In the File gadget enter a suitable filename, ie TestIcon.info. Select the Save gadget. Open the Ram Disk window to see the icon in its full glory!

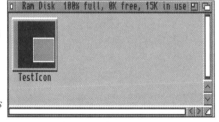

To use your new design ensure the Workbench disk is in the internal drive and enter the following line of AmigaDOS, either via the Execute Command option or in the AmigaShell:

COPY FROM DF0:Utilities/More TO RAM:TestIcon

Now if you double-click on the TestIcon icon you will find that More has been launched. This is because in the copying process we renamed More to TestIcon. When the TestIcon was double-clicked on, it looked for a tool called TestIcon, found it, and ran it!

in the top righthand corner of the IconEdit window. Keep glancing across at this to see if your magnified design is making visual sense at the reduced size.

15

Put the power of your AmigaDOS scripts into the
friendly Workbench environment with IconX.

Plus some example scripts with which you can try
out your programming skills.

*B*eing able to run a program from the Workbench
requires that it has an icon to represent it. As should be
apparent from your understanding of the Workbench
disk there are a lot more directories and files on it than are
actually displayed in the Workbench disk window when it is
opened.

But what do you do if you want to run an AmigaDOS script
from the Workbench? You now have the basic knowledge to
create a simple AmigaDOS script using ED and you also know
how to create and edit an icon using IconEdit. The question is:
How do I tie the two together so that when I click on the icon it
will run the script? The answer might at first sight seem to be
simply ensuring that the script and the icon have a similar
name, and that the icon has the .info postfix. The correct
answer is that it isn't that simple and that to run a script from
the Workbench via an icon you must use a special AmigaDOS
tool file called ICONX.

ICONX

Although it is located in the C directory along with all the AmigaDOS commands, ICONX isn't a command, it is a tool which can be used to assist in the running and managing of files. In this instance ICONX provides the means to allow your own script files to be run and executed from the Workbench by clicking on the icons that you have chosen to associate them with.

The icon .info file that you use in this case is important, as it must allow you to define the default tool used by the program it is to run. This information can be found in the Info box associated with the icon. In other words select the icon concerned and then select the Information option from the Workbench Icon Menu. However, this process requires a much more detailed knowledge of the workings of the Workbench than we will go into here. The simplest method is to use the icon file associated with the Shell.

First create a simple script file that can be used as the worked example. As always, whenever trying out a new technique or idea, keep everything simple to ensure that you don't make any errors. Then once you have mastered the particular technique you can go for it!

Use ED to create the following file:

```
CD RAM:
ED Script
```

Now enter the following three lines into the file:

```
ECHO "Script - the DIY Workbench Script File"
DIR DIRS
ECHO "The End - Returning to the Workbench"
```

Copy the Shell.info file across from the Workbench disk to the Ram Disk and rename this Tester.info:

```
COPY FROM DF0:System/Shell.info TO RAM:Script.info
```

(Note: Under Workbench 2.0 omit System/ from the above command line as Shell.info is stored in the root directory of the Workbench disk.)

If you open the Ram Disk window you will find that the standard Shell icon is in position but is called Tester. Select this by clicking on it once only and open the Info box available from the Workbench menu. The Default Tool will be set to:

Insider Guide #46: Attaching ICONX to a script.

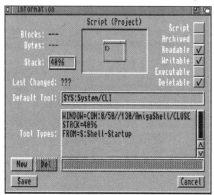

You can run an AmigaDOS script using an icon by attaching the icon assigned to the script to ICONX. The script becomes the project and ICONX the tool to run it.

Copy the Shell icon file, renaming it as the .info file for the script.

Select the new script icon and then choose the Information option from the Icons menu.

Locate the Default tool – this will have SYS:System/CLI defined as the default tool. Click in this string gadget and delete the contents.

Enter the new default tool as:

C:ICONX

Click the Save gadget to confirm your settings.

Double-click on the new icon to run the script using ICONX.

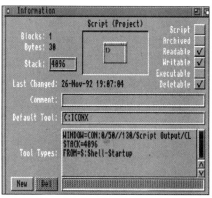

Under Workbench2.1 a number of Tool Types have been defined for you. Before saving click on the one starting WINDOW= to bring it into the string gadget at the bottom.

Edit the size and name accordingly, ie:

WINDOW=CON:100/100/425/100/Script/CLOSE

Under Workbench 2.0 select NEW and then enter the above before you save. Double click on the script icon to run it.

SYS:System/CLI

Click in this box to insert the cursor, delete the line and type this:

C:ICONX

Select Save and then run the Tester script file by double-clicking on the newly created icon. The ICONX window will be opened on screen and the script file will be executed within it.

The script file has run its course inside a standard Shell window. However, it is generally much neater to specify your own window as this can then be made of the correct size to suit your requirements, be positioned on the screen at the point you wish and have the title of your choice. This can be done, but you will first need to call up the Icons Info box as described above if it is not already available.

Under Workbench 2.1 much of this work has already been done for you. In the Tool Types window there should be a definition along the lines of:

WINDOW=CON:0/50//130/AmigaShell/CLOSE

If you click on this it will be displayed in the string gadget underneath. If you are using Workbench 2.0 or this definition is not already available then click on the NEW gadget and then enter – or edit – the text so that it reads:

WINDOW=CON:100/100/425/100/Script/CLOSE

Note that it is important that the first word WINDOW= is entered in capital letters otherwise it will not work. What you have done here is to inform the IconX handler that you wish to use your own window details. Save this and then double-click on the Script icon. Now IconX will run the Script script inside the Shell just defined, roughly central on the screen.

You can add a second TOOLTYPE command should you so wish. The command DELAY allows you to determine how long the window stays open on screen. For example, to set a delay of ten seconds from completing the script file to closing the window, add the following to the TOOLTYPES:

DELAY=600

DELAY works in units of 1/60th of a second, therefore this will cause a delay of ten seconds. If you prefer you can enter:

DELAY=0

and then the window will remain open until you press <Ctrl-C>.

Pass Parameter

AmigaDOS provides you with the ability to pass parameters to script files when they are executed from the command line. The parameters are included on the command line and obviously after the command name. For example, a script file called *Test* might expect two parameters to be passed to it and could therefore be executed with:

```
EXECUTE TEST Today Tonight
```

or if you have set the script flag of the command:

```
TEST Today Tonight
```

Extending this capability to your script files is quite straightforward and requires the inclusion of *key variables* at the start of the file. Key variables take the form:

```
.key <varONE>,[<varTWO>,<etc>]
```

The start of the script file must start with a *.key* – this is very important and there must be no space before it. This must then be followed with the names of the variables you wish to hold the information that is to be passed into it. The term *variable* is applied to special containers which can be used to hold information and you can have as many of these as you can fit on the line, each separated by a comma. The only rule to remember here is that the variable names must be positioned either side of the comma – there should not be any spaces, otherwise AmigaDOS will assume that there are no more variables to come, regardless of whether there are or not!

In the example of TEST given above, the first variable in the list (typically varONE) would be used to hold *Today* and the second defined variable name (typically varTWO) would be used to hold *Tonight*. Note that the variable names you use are arbitrary – use what you wish – and these names do not change. What does change is the information that can be placed into them, thus the term variables. Try this following example:

Use ED and the Ram Disk to create a simple text file containing the following four lines:

```
.key name1, name2
ECHO "The first name was <name1>"
ECHO "The second name was <name2>"
ECHO "Hello <name1> and <name2>!"
```

The variable names are inserted into the program at the desired position and are identified as variables rather than commands or tests by being enclosed within the chevron brackets < and >. As the example shows, they can be used in the program more than once, in fact as many times as needed. Set the file's script flag to allow AmigaDOS to execute it correctly:

```
PROTECT Test S ADD
```

and then run the program passing a couple of names to it en route separating each by a single space:

```
TEST Marc Sarah
```

The reply will come back as follows:

```
The first name was Marc

The second name was Sarah

Hello Marc and Sarah!
```

This principle can be applied to any AmigaDOS command that requires information to be supplied by the user. For example, you could jazz up the COPY command by using some screen messages:

```
.key in,out

ECHO "COPYing from <in> to <out>. Please wait.."

COPY FROM <in> TO <out>

ECHO "All done. Call again soon"
```

Assuming you call the file ECOPY (Easy COPY), you could copy the ED file from the Workbench disk to the Ram Disk in the following way:

```
ECOPY DF0:C/ED RAM:
```

Key Dollars

The above examples are fine, but what if you run the program without passing any parameters? Well that will depend on the program, but it will still run. Any information that is left out will *set* the associated variables with a *null string*, which means just that – nothing!

An alternative way around this is to end a predetermined default using the $ character. For instance, in the first example given you might put default values in the following way:

```
.key <name1>,<name2>
ECHO "The first name was <name1 $ not given>"
ECHO "The second name was <name2 $ not given>"
ECHO "Hello <name1$not given> and <name2$not given>!"
```

Now, if one or both variables are not supplied with information the text after the $ and up until the closing angular bracket will be used instead.

The other scenario that might arise is where too many items are passed as parameters for a command. In this case AmigaDOS will generate an error message. For example using:

```
TEST Marc Sarah Tessie
```

would in this example return:

```
EXECUTE: Parameters unsuitable for key "name1,name2"
```

Key Options

The ability to be able to *take it or leave it* is useful, but it may also be a hindrance. You may want the information and two options are available for use within a key definition to allow you to make a key variable optional or compulsory. The two options are:

Option	Effect
a	Required argument (compulsory)
k	Keyword (optional)

These options can be embedded into the key definition separated from (and after) the variable name by a slash character. For example:

```
.key Name1/a,Name2/k
```

In the above example *Name1* is compulsory and must be supplied, but *Name2* is optional and may be be ignored.

To see how this works start a new Ram Disk based ED file called NAMES and enter the following few lines:

```
.key Name1/a,Name2/k
ECHO "Name one was <Name1>"
ECHO "Name two was <Name2>"
```

Run this first with:

```
EXECUTE NAMES Marc
```

the program will respond with:

```
Name one was Marc

Name two was
```

Trying:

```
EXECUTE NAMES
```

will create an error message because the compulsory parameter has not been included. Try:

```
EXECUTE NAMES Marc Sarah
```

This will also cause an error. The reason is that to use an optional variable you must specify the name of the variable and then follow it by the value to be assigned to it. For example:

```
EXECUTE NAMES Marc Name2 Sarah
```

will respond correctly:

```
Name one was Marc

Name two was Sarah
```

This might appear to be daft at first sight but there is a good reason. Consider the NAMES program which has been extended to give:

```
.key Name1/a,Name2/k,Name3/k

ECHO "Name one was <Name1>"

ECHO "Name two was <Name2>"

ECHO "Name three was <Name3>"
```

In this scenario there are two optional variables, now it becomes imperative to be able to distinguish between them, particularly as you wish to pass information to the variable Name3 and not Name2. For instance:

```
EXECUTE NAMES Marc Name3 Sarah
```

This will produce:

```
Name one was Marc

Name two was

Name three was Sarah
```

The reason and importance for having to be able to specify optional variable names is clearly important. Note that the $ facility is not available to a variable that is defined as a keyword.

Key Variables

We saw above that if a value is not passed on the command line to any particular variable, then it can have a default used with the aid of the dollar operator, $. This is fine but it has drawbacks. If you wish to use the variable several times in the body of a program then you must also insert the default message at each point as appropriate – tiresome.

Also, we have not discovered any mechanism for allowing variables to be defined within the body of the script file. The .DEF function overcomes this. The following short script (called MESSAGE) illustrates how it can be incorporated into the body of a program:

```
.KEY message
; define default message
.DEF message = "non existent!"
; now echo it to screen
ECHO "Message was <message>"
```

Now execute this:

```
EXECUTE MESSAGE
```

and the following will be printed on screen:

```
Message was non existent!
```

But if you supply a parameter on the command line as follows:

```
EXECUTE MESSAGE all right!
```

Then the following will be printed:

```
Message was all right!
```

The DEF function is intelligent, it tests to see if the .KEY variable is empty and if so assigns the new value. If the variable is not empty, ie it had some information passed to it from the command line, it leaves it well alone.

Variables can be defined in programs using this method, however the variable must first be defined with .KEY whether you intend to pass it information or not. The following program, called CONSTANT, demonstrates how this would work:

```
.KEY one,two,three
; Now define constants
.DEF one="ONE (1)"
.DEF two="TWO (2)"
.DEF three="THREE (3)"
ECHO "<one>, <two>, <three>"
```

When executed this will produce:

```
ONE (1), TWO (2), THREE (3)
```

As easy as one, two three!

16

The best possible combination is a mixture of Workbench and AmigaDOS. In fact the use of just a few AmigaDOS commands can make your work load so much lighter.

Read on to find out which ones!

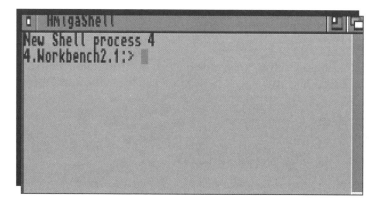

I've mentioned in a few places before now that the best possible use of your Amiga is made by using a combination of Workbench and AmigaDOS. This chapter is a look at some of those particular AmigaDOS commands which you will find very useful when working from the Workbench.

Resident DOS

One particular problem that you will always encounter, especially when using a single disk drive, is the need to continually have to replace the Workbench disk whenever you wish to do something. As you may recall, the main reason for this is that AmigaDOS commands are stored as transient command files on disk. For example, when you type DIR at the AmigaShell (or for that matter open a disk window from the Desktop) AmigaDOS looks in the C: assignment (usually the C directory on the Workbench disk), finds the file called DIR and then loads this into memory before executing it. Once the command has completed its task, AmigaDOS forgets about it. Clearly the whole process of command execution could be speeded up if the command was retained in memory, thereby obviating the need to load it into memory each time it is needed. This can also be an advantage with a dual floppy drive system. The Shell RESIDENT command allows this and has the following syntax:

```
RESIDENT <filename>
```

The DIR command can be made resident by issuing the following command:

```
RESIDENT C:DIR
```

Note that RESIDENT does not know where to look for the file, so the full file path should be given unless the file is in the current directory. To see that DIR is now truly memory resident, catalogue the Ram Disk with:

```
DIR RAM:
```

and notice that the Workbench disk is not accessed at all and also how much quicker the whole process has become.

Note that not all commands can be made resident. However most of the files in the Workbench C directory (that is the directory that contains most of the AmigaDOS commands) can be used. If a program cannot be made resident it will not be loaded and a message to that effect will be displayed.

If you forget which files are currently resident you can obtain a list of them simply by typing:

```
RESIDENT
```

on its own. AmigaDOS will then display a list of the commands currently installed in memory. This will also display a list of all internal commands.

If you wish to remove a command from memory, ie make it non-resident, then use the command with the option REMOVE tagged onto the end. For example, to remove LIST from the resident list (assuming it has been made resident in the first place):

```
RESIDENT LIST REMOVE
```

AmigaDOS internal commands cannot be removed in this way. However, they can be disabled by using the REMOVE option and this is reflected in the RESIDENT list. Note that once a command has been disabled in this way it cannot be re-enabled other than by rebooting the machine.

Prompt Ideas

You can customise the AmigaShell prompt to display information to suit your very own needs using the PROMPT command, which has the following syntax:

```
PROMPT <name>
```

In AmigaDOS two special pseudo-variables are defined as follows:

%n   Display the CLI number.

%s   Display current directory path.

The default value of PROMPT is:

```
PROMPT %n.%s>
```

If you wish to display only the current directory path and not the window number, you can issue:

```
PROMPT %s>
```

Text can also be incorporated freely as part of the prompt definition. For example:

```
PROMPT "Shell %n >"
```

would display a prompt which looks a bit like this:

```
Shell 1 >
```

Note that if you wish to include spaces as part of the PROMPT command definition you must enclose the entire text within double quotes.

Alias AmigaDOS

You will probably already be aware that some AmigaDOS commands can become quite long and involved. Even relatively short commands can become tedious to enter and re-enter if you are using them frequently. AmigaDOS provides a command that allows you to rename other commands, making it possible to give even the longest and most complex of command sequences a one letter name! The command in question is called ALIAS and it takes the following form:

```
ALIAS <new command> <existing command>
```

Let's look at a few simple examples first. Changing between DF0: and the Ram Disk involves two words apiece, namely:

```
CD DF0:
CD RAM:
```

We could make aliases for both of these. To do this, first decide on the new command aliases you wish to apply to each one. C0 and CR for C(hange to DF0: and C(hange to) R(am Disk) might be appropriate, therefore:

```
ALIAS C0 CD DF0:
ALIAS CR CD RAM:
```

Typing CR or C0 will now have the desired effect.

```
ALIAS D0 DIR DF0:
ALIAS DR DIR RAM:
```

could also be used to make the cataloguing of the Ram Disk and DF0: that bit easier.

If you find yourself continually swapping between two directories on a disk drive, say the Utilities and the System directories, this could be catered for as follows:

```
ALIAS UTLS CD DF0:Utilities
ALIAS SYST CD DF0:System
```

In particular, a well arranged and well structured disk hierarchy may allow you to find files on it quickly, but at the expense of long CD commands. The ALIAS command allows you to assign a simple name of your choosing to the most complex of commands.

Some commands such as COPY require the inclusion of parameters which will always change. This has been catered for by allowing the [] (square brackets) combination to inform AmigaDOS that a parameter will be passed at this point. For example, let's create a command that will always copy a file to the Ram Disk from the current disk drive. The name CRAM (Copy RAM) will be used as the alias:

```
ALIAS CRAM COPY FROM [ ] TO RAM:
```

To copy the Shell file to the Ram Disk we could use:

```
CRAM Shell
```

To copy a file from any device, simply include the device name as per normal:

```
CRAM DF1:Test
```

would copy a file called Test from the disk in DF1:. If you wish to see a list of current ALIAS commands just type ALIAS by itself. When you do this you will see a number of extra aliases. These are in fact used by AmigaDOS itself.

One point to remember about ALIAS commands is that they are Shell specific. An ALIAS command created in one Shell is not available for use in any other Shell.

If you are using Workbench 2.1 and would like to have the REVERSE and NORMAL commands outlined in Chapter Seven then you can define them with the following ALIAS commands:

```
alias reverse "echo *"*E[>1m*E[30;41m*E[0;0H*E[J*""
alias normal "echo *"*E[>0m*E[31;40m*E[0;0H*E[J*""
```

New Shells

As you learn to customise your own work disks (covered in Chapter 22) you will invariably find the need to open additional Shell windows. Without the Workbench loaded there is no access to the Shell icon interface to do this. The NEWSHELL command is provided for this purpose.

The syntax of the command is:

```
NEWSHELL NEWCON:<x/y/width/height/name>
```

Try this example for yourself:

```
NEWSHELL NEWCON:10/10/500/100/SecondShell
```

A second Shell window will appear covering most of the top of the screen, leaving enough space to the right to allow the Workbench icons to be displayed. The title SecondShell will be displayed along with the following inside the Shell itself:

```
New Shell process 2
Workbench2:>
```

This Shell is now the active Shell and any typing will now appear inside this window until another is selected. This window could be used to allow direct access to the Ram Disk by typing:

CD RAM:

You will now effectively have a window on the Ram Disk and one on the internal drive. Handy in itself. To close a Shell window, use the ENDCLI command – remember that this must be typed into the window that you wish to close.

Assigned Path

You will probably now already have realised the tedium that can come with having to type and retype long directory path roots. While the use of the Shell's editing facilities alleviate this to some degree, long path roots can become the proverbial pain in the perineum. The command ASSIGN can be used to simplify access to various locations.

We used an example of the ALIAS command earlier in this book to assign a short name to a long path name, however ALIAS forms part of the Shell and can only be used from within it. It is no good unless you are running the application or program from that Shell. ASSIGN solves this problem in one fell swoop and has the added advantage in that it may be included in your startup and script files as required. The syntax of the command is:

ASSIGN <name> <path>

If you found yourself continually having to access two directories in the Ram Disk which had the tedious paths:

RAM:Projects/Book/TextFiles/Edit

RAM:Projects/Book/TextFiles/UnEd

then you could simply assign a name to each of them as follows:

ASSIGN Better: RAM:Projects/Book/TextFiles/Edit

ASSIGN Original: RAM:Projects/Book/TextFiles/UnEd

Then if you wanted to load a file called ChapOne from RAM:Projects/Book/TextFiles/UnEdited you could do so simply by using Original:ChapOne as the file name.

Finally if you wish to see what names the Workbench assigns to various paths and devices you can do so by typing:

ASSIGN

on its own.

17

**Card sharks will recognise the term *Jokers Wild*
and we can apply the same principle to file
management on the A600.**

**Read on for enlightenment on the many clever
ways to copy.**

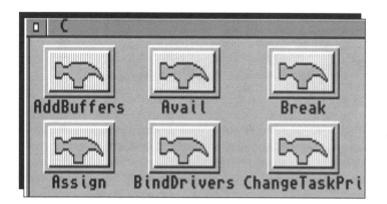

*I*f you are looking to copy a block of files then clearly using
the Workbench would look to be the simplest option. You
can group the files together, lasso them using the marquee
technique and then drag them into the destination window.
But the problem is that this will only work with files that have
icons associated with them. What do you do if you want to
copy files that do not have icons associated with them? Well
there are in fact two options. The main one is what this chapter
is primarily about and involves the use of AmigaDOS. The
other still involves the use of the Workbench!

If you reveal the Workbench menu bar and look at the Window
menu you will notice that one of the options is Show. If you
move down to this you will reveal a submenu which has two
further options. These are:

    Only Icons

    All Files

By default the Only Icons option is invoked – therefore you only see files that have icons associated with them. However if you select the Show All Files option then every single file in the drawers, whether it has a .info file associated with it or not, will be displayed. The default icon for the particular type of file is used.

By using this option to force all files to be displayed you can than select and copy them in the normal Workbench fashion, before re-selecting the Only Icons option to revert the display to a less cluttered one.

Jokers Wild

If you have ever played any card games you may have occasionally used the rule where *Jokers are wild*. The Jokers are left in the pack of cards and if you are dealt one it can be used to represent any card you wish. Filename wildcards work in much the same way. Certain characters can be used within filenames to represent any character or set of characters you may wish. The two most common combinations are:

?   Represents any single character

#?   Represents any pattern of any characters

The latter option is clearly the most powerful, particularly when you wish to copy or delete a whole range of files.

The #? sequence can be used to copy a whole directory of files. For instance we could move the entire contents of the Workbench Utilities directory into the Ram Disk by using the following command:

COPY FROM SYS:Utilities/#? TO RAM:

When you type this into the Shell the copy will take place. As COPY encounters each file in the Utilities directory it displays its name in the Shell window and then prints *copied* when it has finished transferring it.

If you wished, you could suppress this filename by using the QUIET option. This is easy to use as you just append it to the end of the command. Thus the example given above becomes:

COPY FROM SYS:Utilities/#? TO RAM: QUIET

If you reopen the Ram Disk window you will see the utilities are in place.

Insider Guide #47: Using Show All Files to Copy.

Selecting the Show All Files option from the Window menu will reveal all other files and directories present.

Here, when applied to the Workbench2.1 disk, it reveals three new drawers called C, L and Libs.

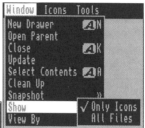

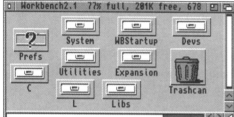

The C drawer holds the AmigaDOS commands – opening this will reveal them all. Each uses the default hammerhead icon for display because they are all tools.

You can use the standard Workbench selection methods to copy files that would not otherwise be seen using this simple but very effective technique.

When you have finished just select Show Only Icons from the Windows

The same wildcard could be used to delete the files from the Ram Disk. The syntax for this is:

```
DELETE RAM:#?
```

Try this and each file name will be displayed as it is deleted.

The *original* Ram Disk directories will not be deleted as they are being used by AmigaDOS and a message to this effect is displayed. One or two files might remain because they are *protected from deletion*. Don't worry if this happens.

In this form the COPY and DELETE commands are fairly robust but it is possible to be a bit more selective. Imagine that we wish to copy just the Clock files across from the Utilities directory. We know that the two files have the word *Clock* in common, therefore we can use the following COPY command:

```
COPY FROM SYS:Utilities/Clock#? TO RAM:
```

The #? combination can be used at any point in the filename. For example:

```
COPY FROM SYS:Utilities/#?.info TO RAM:
```

would copy all the .info files from the Utilities directory to the Ram Disk.

The same technique can also be used to delete files but extreme care must be taken as you may also delete other files starting with Clock. However there is a way around this and similar sorts of problems as we shall see below. However, if in doubt do it manually, file by file – better safe than sorry!

By using ? as a wildcard you can be a shade more selective. For example you may have a disk containing some chapters of a book created in a wordprocessor. These may be called CHAP1, CHAP2, CHAP3 etc. To copy the lot in one go we could use the ? wildcard in the position of the character that changes – the CHAP number, thus:

```
COPY FROM DF0:CHAP? TO RAM:
```

It is also possible to use more than one ? in the command, in fact you could use as many as you wished. The following example would copy all files which have filenames of four characters:

```
COPY FROM DF0:???? TO RAM:
```

A practical example would be:

```
COPY FROM DF0:Utilities/???? TO RAM:
```

which would copy the MORE file into the Ram Disk as the only file with four characters in its name.

This 'n' That

In an earlier chapter we saw that some files have *extensions* tagged onto them to make it clear what type of file they are. Prime examples are the .info files associated with the various icons. Wordprocessor files might be distinguished by having .doc appended to them and some versions of BASIC for the Amiga use the extension .BAS. If we wished to copy all the .info and .BAS files to the Ram Disk from a disk in drive DF0: we could use the following:

```
COPY FROM DF0:#?.INFO TO RAM:
```

```
COPY FROM DF0:#?.BAS TO RAM:
```

This can be simplified using the I option (this is called the double-bar and appears on the \ key when using the gb keymap).

What we wish to do is to copy any files that end with .INFO or .BAS. This would be entered as follows:

```
COPY FROM DFO:#?.(INFO|BAS) TO RAM:
```

As both extensions contain a dot this can be left outside the parentheses which are used to include the variable OR options.

Let's try a more practical example using the Workbench disk you booted with. Let's copy all the files from the root directory that end with t or e. The command is:

```
COPY FROM S:#?(t|e) TO RAM:
```

The format, as with all wildcards, is free form and so it is possible to include it as the start of a filename. Thus to copy all the files that begin with E or P use:

```
COPY FROM DFO:(E|P)#? TO RAM:
```

Advanced Pattern Matching

Now that you know what the wildcards do, we'll look at how they work. We've said, ? matches any single character and #? matches any group of characters. Why? It works like this:

#X	matches any repeating sequence of character X
?	matches any character.

therefore:

#?	matches any sequence of any character (anything)

Pattern matching stops when any non-wildcard character string is encountered – just about anything in other words – but can be restarted at any point. This means that you can specify patterns like:

This Matches		These
AB#?D	=	ABCD, ABCCD, ABxQvD
Mast#?.1.#?	=	Mastering DOS2.1.DOC
A??B#?D	=	AeeBxxxxD, AAABzD, A12B3456D

Using parentheses, you can group patterns or wildcards together:

A(B|C)D	=	ABD, acd

A(#B|C)D	=	ABD, ABBD, ABBBBD, AbbbbbD, ACD
A(B|C?)D	=	ABD, ACD, Ac1d, ACaD

But what if you wanted to get at a file which includes a pattern matching character? This is achieved using the tick symbol (') which disables the wildcard which follows it. If you need to get at a file with more than one wildcard, you must use a tick for each. Tick itself can be matched using two ticks!

A'?B	=	A?B
A'#B	=	A#B
A'#'?B	=	A#?B
A''B	=	A'B

There is also a special pattern matching character called NOT. The tilde symbol (~) is used for this and just reverses the action of the pattern. Strange at first, sure, but incredibly useful once you get used to it:

~#?	=	Nothing!
~(#?.info)	=	Everything but dot-info files
~(.info|.pat)	=	Everything except dot-info and dot-pat files.

File Info

When a new directory or file is created, or indeed when a file is updated, AmigaDOS saves various bits of information about it and these bits of information are referred to as its attributes. The easiest way to see the attributes of some files is to use the command LIST. Try this using your Workbench disk. Make your AmigaShell window as wide as possible first of all as the information supplied uses the full width of the screen. The information listed provides the following information:

```
<Filename><length><flags><date created> <time created>
<Filenote..........>
```

Consider the following two *sample* files displayed with LIST:

```
Letters Dir     - - rwed   01-Jan-91  17:02:00
Memo    405     - - rwed   01-Jan-91  17:12:23
```

Letters is a directory signified by the fact that it has Dir in the second column. The third column (--rwed) is a list of flags and these signify more advanced information about the file. The date and time follow and show that the *Letters* directory was created on 1st January 1991 at 5:02pm.

Memo is a file (as opposed to a Dir) which is 405 bytes long. It has the same flags status as *Letters* and was created on the same day at 5:12:23pm.

If you list the contents of a disk and find that the date is not given – it gives day names and terms such as *Future* then it is likely that you have not set the date on your system. This is done with the DATE command which has the following syntax:

```
DATE [DD-MMM-YY] [HH:MM:SS]
```

As you can see both the date and time are entirely optional and typing DATE on its own returns the current date and time being used by the system. Unless you have a battery backed clock installed this is likely to be incorrect. Here are some legal examples of DATE:

```
DATE 01-Jan-90 17:00:00
DATE 01-Dec-91
DATE 12:00:00
DATE 12:34:56
```

Note that the inclusion of a seconds value is optional. If you do not have a battery backed clock system then setting the DATE will still work and be available while the machine is switched on. Like the Ram Disk the contents of the internal clock will be lost, however, when the machine is switched off.

The last item of information that might be supplied is <Filenote>. This is a comment which can be saved with the file or directory, and which is displayed with LIST. The note itself can be up to 79 characters in length and if used sensibly can save a lot of time when you are trying to locate a particular file or directory. The command FILENOTE attaches the comment to the file/directory and it has the following syntax:

```
FILENOTE <filename> COMMENT '<filenote>'
```

For example, copy the Shell from the Workbench disk into the Ram Disk and then add a filenote to it thus:

```
FILENOTE RAM:Shell.info COMMENT 'The Shell'
```

On a subsequent LIST this might be displayed thus:

```
Shell.info Dir   - - rwed    01-Jan- 90 12:34:50
: The Shell
```

The filenote is distinguished by being preceded with a colon.

Printers are one of the first add-ons you are
likely to buy for your Amiga. But just getting the
two to talk to each other can be a real pain.

See how to select a printer driver and use the
Amiga's printer preferences to get access to your
own printed word.

```
Printer Preferences

        Printer Type                  Printer Port: [▷]    Parallel
 EpsonQ                               Print Pitch:  [▷]  Pica (10 cpi)
 EpsonX                              Print Spacing: [▷] 6 Lines Per Inch
 EpsonXOld                           Print Quality: [▷]     Draft
 generic
                                       Paper Type:  [▷]   Continuous
                                      Paper Format: [▷] Narrow Tractor

                                     Paper Length (lines)    : [66]
                                     Left Margin (characters): [5]
 EpsonQ                              Right Margin (characters): [75]
```

*T*rying to deal with printers within a chapter or two of a
book about the Workbench and AmigaDOS is a thank-
less task. No, perhaps that's the wrong phrase – it's a difficult task. The bottom line is that there is so much to write
about that printers need a book on their own. Indeed,
Mastering Amiga Printers is a sister volume available to meet
just that requirement. So for the purposes of this book we'll
limit ourselves to the bare necessities of printer usage and how
to set a printer up from the Workbench using the various
Preference editors available for that purpose. For a more complete guide to using, choosing and troubleshooting I'll refer you
once again to Robin Burton's wonderful tome *(see Appendix B)*.

One point to bear in mind at the very off here is that while solving printer problems may be infuriating, do remember that one
of the best ways of solving them is to experiment. By obtaining
printed output at each stage you should be able to see what
actions have what effect.

Printer Types

While there are quite literally hundreds of printers to choose from, it is important to remember that there are also different types of printers from which you can make your selection. The distinction is important because the type of printer determines the way in which the printer produces its final printed output. At the time of writing these are the most common printer technologies:

Daisywheel

Dot-matrix 9-pin

Dot-matrix 24-pin

Inkjet

Laser

Thermal

Of these the dot-matrix technology is certainly the most popular, not least because of its versatility but also because of its cost effectiveness. Certainly from the Amiga point of view it is probably the type that is connected 99% of the time and generally it is the printer type the Amiga is geared towards when it comes to use the Preferences editor PrinterGFX.

You connect your printer to your Amiga via a cable that is connected at the printer port. This can be either a parallel port or a serial port. Again, both are available but 99% of the time, and with a dot-matrix printer 99.9% of the time, it will be through the parallel printer port. Within the Amiga these ports are referred to by the volume names PAR: and SER:. These two volume names represent the lowest (crudest if you like) level you can address your printer manually. Normally when working directly through the Desktop you will have little need to reference these unless you are using the AmigaShell interface.

In addition to PAR: and SER: there is another nominal device called PRT:, a contraction of the word printer. Normally, this would be the lowest level at which you would address the printer because it will normally be aligned with PAR: or SER: as appropriate. PRT: should know to what printer port your printer is connected if you have defined your Workbench preferences correctly.

The Amiga, and that includes Workbench and every other program or application you may run, knows how to talk to your printer because it follows a predefined set of rules for operation. This is more complex than it might seem at first sight because there are so many different models and types of printer and each differs from the other, not only in physical shape but also in the facilities they have to offer you as the user. Trying to write a single piece of software for the Amiga that can take into account these differences and also cater for all eventualities would be nigh on impossible. Therefore, it is common for separate printer driving programs to be supplied, each of which is custom written to do the right job for the right printer. This is called the printer driver and several are supplied with the Workbench, many more are available from a variety of sources – such as PD Libraries – and you just install the correct one for your printer as part of printer preferences.

Now that we have got a few of the basics out of the way, and we'll assume that you have connected your printer to your Amiga at the relevant point, let's see how we get it up and running. Assuming you are using a dot-matrix printer, there are three essential steps to take:

1.   Choose and install the correct printer driver.

2.   Define the system defaults.

3.   Define graphics defaults.

We'll look at each of these in turn.

Printer Driver

As always you should be working with a backup copy of your Workbench disk. The main task is to select a printer driver from those that are supplied on the Extras disk and copy this to the relevant point on the Workbench disk. That relevant point is the DEVS/PRINTERS directory on the Workbench disk.

If you have bought a popular make of printer and have taken advice from a friend or dealer then you may already be pretty sure as to the identity of the printer driver you are going to use.

Chances are its name will stand out for you. If at the end of the day you're stuck, you probably need to experiment using the various printer drivers to hand. For instance, Star, Panasonic, Taxan, Citizen, Mannesman and many others are all highly Epson compatible so an Epson driver will do the job. The bottom line is to buy a printer which you have a printer driver available for – or a combination you know works. Common sense really. Here is a list of the more common printer drivers which are supplied as part of Workbench 2.1:

CalComp_ColorMaster	CalComp_ColorMaster2
CanonBJ10	CBM_MPS1000
Diablo_630	EpsonQ
EpsonX	EpsonXOld
Howtek_Pixelmaster	HP_DeskJet
HP_DeskJetOld	HP_LaserJet
HP_PaintJet	HP_ThinkJet
ImagewriterII	NEC_Pinwriter
Okidata_293	Okidata_92
Okimate_20	PostScript
Seiko_5300	Seiko_5300a
Sharp_JX-730	Tektronix_4693D
Tektronix_4696	Toshiba_P351C
Toshiba_P351SX	Xerox_4020

Once you have identified the printer driver you need (you can install more than one if you want) you need to copy it from the Extras disk into the **DEVS/PRINTERS** drawer on the Workbench disk.

Under Workbench 2.1 the printer drivers are located in the Storage/Printers drawer (ie in the Printers drawer which is found within the Storage drawer) and they can be seen simply by opening the window on that drawer. Under Workbench 2.04/2.05 they are in the Devs drawer on the Extras disk – however, you will need to use the Shell or the Show All Files option to view the drivers present.

Copying should be straightforward although, if you are using a single drive you may be called upon to swap your Workbench and Extras disks a couple of times. The process for copying other or additional printer drivers is the same.

If you have a dual drive system and want to do the whole process from the AmigaShell, proceed as follows (here copying the EpsonQ printer driver):

Workbench 2.1:

```
COPY FROM Extras2.1:STORAGE/PRINTERS/EpsonQ TO
Workbench2.1:DEVS/PRINTERS
```

Workbench 2.04/2.05:

```
COPY FROM Extras2.0:DEVS/PRINTERS/EpsonQ TO
Workbench2.0:DEVS/PRINTERS
```

Printer Prefs

The Printer Preferences editor is easy to use. It is located in the Prefs drawer on the Extras2.1 disk (or on the Workbench2.0 disk if you are running version 2.04/2.05). When double-clicked a standard Preferences editor window is displayed.

The top righthand corner of the editor window displays the printer drivers available for you to use. By default there is a single printer driver called generic. If you have copied across a printer driver from the Extras disk as outlined above, this should also be listed. The generic printer driver is a general all-purpose interface. In most cases it will allow you to do standard text printing but without too many special effects. Generally you won't use it. You can have numerous printer drivers available to you simply by copying them into the DEVS/PRINTERS directory on your Workbench disk. However, do bear in mind that there is not a lot of spare space on your Workbench disk and every additional printer driver you copy eats into this. As a rule of thumb just limit yourself to the driver you are actually going to use.

The printer driver window is a scrollable window and you can locate the one you need by using the scroll gadgets should the list extend beyond the bands of the window itself. Click on the driver name of your choice once and its name will be displayed in the small window underneath the printer driver list window. This is now the selected driver. Incidentally, you can use this small text string to enter the full path name of a different driver which can be used at that point – it doesn't have to be located in the DEVS/PRINTERS directory.

The Printer Preferences editor window is then divided into three regions, each of which has three further options to make a selection. These mostly use simple cycle gadgets onto which you click to cycle through the available options.

Printer Port allows you to select where the Amiga sends the information to the printer – as outlined at the start of this chapter this will be set to Parallel nine times out of ten, but it can also be set to Serial. PRT: will be set to this.

Paper Type can be either Single of Fan-fold. The former is single sheets of paper whereas the latter is more commonly called continuous computer stationary. The Paper Size option is rather misleading, because it actually refers to the maximum length of the line you will be allowed to print. The default is suitable for most printers which offer an 80-column width. You may need to change this to wide tractor if you are using a wide carriage printer – 132 column for instance. As with many of the settings available here there is nothing to be lost, and indeed a great deal of experience to be gained, simply by trying each option out for yourself and seeing what the result is. The worst you can do is waste a few sheets of paper and if you use the same sheet all the time...

At the top righthand side of the window are three more settings. These are numeric values which you click on to highlight the text gadget and then enter a new value or edit an existing one. The first of these is Paper Length (Lines) which has a default value of 66. For a standard sheet of paper, single sheet or continuous, 66 lines is generally ideal but this is provided you don't change other options – as I said a lot of experimentation to suit your own needs!. Left Margin (Chars) is the number of characters in from the left where the printer will start printing. Similarly Right Margin (Chars) is the position of the right-hand margin of the text, calculated as the number of characters that will be sent to that particular line. Thus for any one line the actual number of characters printed is the Right Margin minus the Left Margin.

Again these figures are always slightly arbitrary, because in the first place it depends where you feed the paper through the printer. You can for instance vary the lefthand margin simply by feeding the paper through the printer further to the left or right. As I keep saying it's all down to you really. Fix a point in your mind's eye where you will feed the paper through – make a mark or set one of the paper guides that some printers have and use this as a reference point. Then if you pre-fer a wide lefthand margin increase this value to suit.

A finer point to bear in mind with regards to margin settings is that in Printer Preferences the left and right margin positions are specified in absolute character numbers starting from character position number one, however character positions in printers always start from zero. This should not be a problem but if you want to be totally accurate you should remember to add one to whatever value the printer manual indicates if you need to transfer printer command settings into Preferences. In other words in an 80 column printer character posi-tions go from 0 to 79, but in Printer Preferences they go from 1 to 80.

Print Pitch has three possible settings, 10, 12 and 15, though only 24-pin printers are likely to offer the latter. Old 9-pin dot matrix printers won't be able to handle it. The values refer to the number of characters printed in one inch of horizontal space. Thus in 10 pitch, there are 10 characters printed per inch across the page. Print Spacing refers to the

Insider Guide #48: Printer Installation.

When the Printer Preferences window is displayed it will list any printer drivers that have already been copied into the Devs directory.

You can copy as many as you wish.

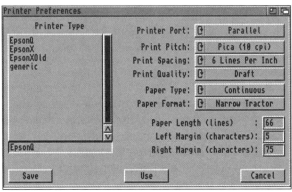

To select a printer driver just click on its name in the scroll window so that it is displayed in the string gadget underneath.

You can use the other gadgets to select specific settings relating to your own requirements as described in the text.

Before you use your settings you must initialise the printer by double-clicking on the InitPrinter icon to be found in the Tools drawer.

number of lines printed per vertical inch of space – the default is 6lpi – that's 6 lines per inch. The higher the number here the less space there is between each line of text. Setting this to say 3 produces well spaced out lines.

Finally, there is Print Quality and there are two options here Draft and Letter. Draft is a lower quality print output but is very much faster to produce and creates less wear and tear on your printer ribbon. Letter is a higher quality more dense output which takes longer to produce and has a wearing effect on the printer ribbon. For general purpose output use Draft and switch to Letter as and when you need it.

Backtracking a bit to the subject of spacing. When we talk of spaces we refer to the width of printed spaces, but the actual size of the space depends on the character size currently being used. A space is bigger in 10 pitch than it is in 12 pitch. If you set your printer's margins in Printer Preferences they're actually the real printer margins, but their physical positions will always depend on the typesize you have set in Printer Preferences.

Printer Init

The offshoot of this is that if you later change the printer's character size and reinitialise the printer to force the changes into effect, unless you have adjusted the left and right margin values accordingly too, the printer's physical margins will move!

Once you have set the Printer Preferences to meet your requirements that is not the end of the story. All that has happened at this point is that the settings you chose have been saved on the Workbench disk as part of your preferences setup. The printer hasn't got the foggiest idea about what you have done – yet! To send this setting to the printer requires the use of InitPrinter, which is located in the Tools drawer. Its use is ultra simple. Firstly turn on your printer and ensure that it is on-line. This is usually signified by a small light being illuminated on the front panel of the printer and basically means that the printer is listening out for information from the computer it is connected to. Secondly double-click on the InitPrinter icon. And that's it. All being well your printer is now set up as you defined in your Printer Preferences.

A couple of points to bear in mind here. If you change any of the settings in Printer Preferences you have to send them to your printer. The best way to do this is to rest the printer – turn it off for a few seconds and then switch it back on before running InitPrinter again. Also, many modern printers have a control panel now which allows you to make specific changes at the printer itself – these will override any previous values sent by InitPrinter.

Serial Change

Primarily we have dealt with the use of a parallel printer – this will be the case most of the time – but it is possible to use a serial printer with the Amiga. For the most part the Printer Preferences will stay the same with the exception of the fact that Printer Port will need to be set to Serial.

It is important that your Serial Preferences settings are correct for your printer. A typical setting for a fairly standard serial printer would go like this:

Handshaking DTR and RTS/CTS

Data Word

1 start bit

8 data bits

Odd, even or no parity

1 or more stop bits

The exact information for your serial printer will be supplied in the printer manual. As always don't be afraid to experiment a bit if you find yourself lacking a bit of information. The combinations aren't endless!

PrintFiles

In the Tools drawer you will find a tool called PrintFiles. This provides a most convenient way of sending a series of files to the printer for printing.

If you have a printer attached to your Amiga then you might want to try sending a file to it. For a test run I would suggest that you use a simple text file created using ED and with an icon attached to it using IconX as previously described.

To send a file first depress and keep depressed the Shift key. Next click on the icon you wish to print, and keeping the Shift key depressed double-click on the PrintFiles icon. The file will now be sent to the printer. Note that Workbench does not inform you of the fact – it just gets on and does it! If there is a problem, Workbench will inform you by displaying a System requester.

Note that you can print a whole succession of files at one time should you so wish. To do this locate the files to be printed and copy them to a common location along with the PrintFiles utility. Then select all the files to be printed as outlined above, simply press and keep depressed the Shift key and then select each file in turn. When all files are selected, and with the Shift key still depressed, double-click on the PrintFiles icon.

19

The Amiga is world famous for its superb graphics capabilities. Quite naturally, if you have a printer attached you will want to put screen to paper.

Well you can, by making full use of the Amiga printer graphic preferences.

```
Graphics Printer Preferences
                                              Color
   Dithering:  [↕]     Ordered
                                               Red:
    Scaling:  [↕]     Fraction
                                             Green:
      Image:  [↕]     Positive
                                              Blue:
     Aspect:  [↕]     Horizontal
      Shade:  [↕]   Black & White    Left Edge (in
```

*I*n the last chapter we examined the use of the Printer Preferences editor to control how the Amiga interfaces to a connected printer. Many of the settings in the Printer Preferences are fundamental to successful printer operation and in that respect are essential. There is a further Printer Preferences editor, PrinterGfx, and this is used to control the way in which a suitable printer – such as a standard dot-matrix printer – produces graphic dumps. A graphic dump is a print-out of part of or all of a screen image. If you thought that producing a carbon copy of a screen from your Amiga was a simple matter, think again. The Amiga Workbench can make it a simple matter but there is an awful lot going on in the background!

The PrinterGfx Preferences editor is located in the Prefs drawer of the Extras2.1 disk (or on the Workbench 2.0 disk). When double-clicked it displays a relatively straightforward screen but for a first time user the range and, in particular, the naming of some of the options can be more than a little off-putting.

However, the same basic principle that was laid down in the last chapter – and indeed the basic philosophy of using your Amiga in general – still remains. Don't be afraid to experiment with different settings and see what the results are. Experimentation is the key to getting the very best from your Amiga.

Colour Correct

Being American in origin this is actually labelled Color Correct in the Graphics Printer Preferences window. This option is only of relevance if you have a colour printer and are looking to produce a colour screen dump. What this tries to do is to produce a better match of the screen colours to those on the final printed output. You should bear in mind however that the end results are not going to be perfect. Colour perception is a personal thing and can be affected by monitor brightness, contrast and so forth.

There are three check boxes, R, G and B which stand for the Red, Green and Blue colours. To turn on colour correction you simply check the box of the colour you wish to try and correct. So if you decide that the red in the printed copy doesn't look right, you can check this box. You can check one, two or all three of the boxes but for each box you check there is a reduction in the number of colours the Amiga can actually try and print on your printer. Of course, the result of this might be that the colour is even more off the mark than before, but that's for you to decide! By default and with no corrections, the Amiga should be capable of producing some 4096 different colours – this figure is displayed below the three color correction check boxes. For each colour you enable for correction there is a reduction of 308 in the total number of colours available to you – such is the price of perfection! Of course, this entire option is only available for colour printers!

Dithering

Dithering is on of a handful of cycle gadgets available as a block in the PrinterGfx preferences editor. The option can have one of three settings – Ordered, Halftone and Floyd-Steinberg.

Dithering is a technique which only applies to colour printing, and it plays an important role in the correct representation of colours. In ordered dithering the coloured dots that compose the picture are

Insider Guide #49: PrinterGfx Preferences.

The PrinterGfx Preferences editor allows you to define the way in which your Amiga uses the attached printer to produce graphics dumps.

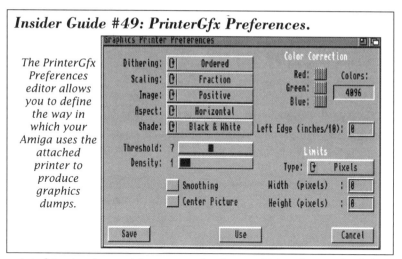

printed in simple, straight rows and columns. Using this method there is a very noticeable regularity to the printing of colour shades. Printing using this setting is the quickest of the three, the penalty for this speed is that the final results can look a bit false.

Halftone dithering is a method of varying both the density and the precise position of the individual coloured dots when mixed colour shades are required. Halftone images therefore appear a little softer and are easier on the eye.

Floyd-Steinberg or F-S dithering, employs a quite complex algorithm to manipulate the physical pixel data from the screen, so that in effect screen colours are slightly smeared before being translated into printer dots. This method of dithering takes time and hence should be limited to final printouts of images.

Sometimes when printing diagonal lines their edges can look jagged. One way to work around this is to check the Smoothing gadget in the PrinterGfx Preferences editor. With this enabled the printing software attempts to reduce the effect by algorithmically manipulating the data before it is translated into printer graphics. This takes some time and therefore with Smoothing enabled print speed is greatly decreased.

Scaling

The final size of your printed image can be affected by the setting of Scaling. There are two options, Fraction and Integer. The final size of the printed image depends on this setting and the printer's line length. This means that you are not just restricted to prints which are in a one-to-one ratio with the screen image.

Fraction, as its name suggests, allows the height and width of the image to be fractionally adjusted so as to maintain the correct overall proportions. This means that, depending on the values set by Limits (see later), individual screen pixels in either plane might be expanded or omitted altogether, so as to preserve the required image proportions.

Integer is the converse of Fraction. In other words every pixel on the screen is guaranteed to be reproduced in the printed output by an even number of dots, and the number will be in the same proportion as the adjustments made to all the other pixels in the printed area.

Limits

This gadget allows you to control the overall size and shape of your printed image. Used in conjunction with Scaling described above, you can create special effects, range the print size and even distort the final output. There are also two text string gadgets which allow you to define the Width and Height of the image to be printed. Click in either of these and delete, edit and enter new numeric values. The units of measurement are tenths of an inch and therefore a setting of:

    Width 60

and:

    Height 40

would give an image of six inches wide by four inches high, subject to the cycle gadget selections under which there are five options available – Bounded, Absolute, Pixels, Multiply and Ignore.

Bounded means that the size of the printed image will not be greater than the Height and Width values defined in the Limits settings (see below). Images may be smaller but not any larger when Bounded is selected.

Absolute can be used in any one of three different ways. If both Height and Width values are supplied the final printed image will be precisely the size specified, regardless of the screen image's true aspect ratio. If only one of the limits is set, either Height or Width, entering zero for the other, the printed image will have the correct aspect ratio while at the same time precisely matching the dimension specified. Thus if 60 is specified as the Width then the width will be six inches and the height will be the correct Height to match the width. The final Absolute option is when both Height and Width are set to zero. In this circumstance the width will be the maximum possible – based on your Printer Preferences – and the height will be in proportion to this.

Pixels works in exactly the same way as Absolute except that the Height and Width values are taken as numbers of pixels rather than tenths of an inch.

Multiply is misleading in that it doesn't allow you to magnify the size of an image in the way you might think. Multiply allows the height and width of the printed image to be adjusted, in proportion to each other if required but based on a ratio. The units used in this case are simple number values, but represent pixels. For instance, if the Width is specified as two and the Height four, then the printed image will be twice the screen's image in width (in pixels) and the printed height will be based on four times the number of pixels on the screen.

With Ignore selected the Width and Height limits are totally ignored and the printed image's size is the size determined by the application that should now be responsible for printing the image.

Image Aspects

Image can be set to Positive or Negative and you can think of the difference between the two like being the difference between a photographic positive and negative. Positive produces a (normal) printer dump while negative swaps the blacks and whites over. It only applies to monochrome images though.

The Aspect setting effectively defines the orientation of the image on the paper. When set to Horizontal the image is printed across the paper as it appears on the screen of the monitor. When set to Vertical the image is printed sideways with what appears at the top of the screen running down the righthand side of the paper. This can be useful when you want to print images that are quite wide so that you can use the full length of the paper.

The Left Offset gadget allows you to define the number of inches to shift (or offset) the image. This is much the same as the Left Margin option in Printer Preferences really. The offset can be defined in steps of tenths of inches, thus a value of 1.5 would be one and one half inches. The Centre Picture gadget allows you to ensure that the printed image is produced centrally on the page. With this gadget checked the Left Offset gadget is inoperative and any values entered will be ignored until Centre Picture is disabled.

Shade

The last of the cycle gadgets, this one has four options which allow you to define what colours to print, or perhaps more correctly, how colours are printed. This option, like many others, is rather dependent on your printer being able to support it. The four options available are Black & White, Grey Scale 1, Grey Scale 2, and Color.

The first option Black & White, when selected, means literally what it says – the image printed will be limited to black and white with no colours being used (this does assume that you are using a ribbon that has a black component in it). This is a useful option to select if you simply want to print out a trial image to check on the picture itself, plus its other components such as size and position.

In contrast to Black & White prints, Grey Scale 1 allows each of the colours on the screen to be printed in a particular shade of grey which best represents the colours on screen. This is achieved by varying the dot-patterns printed. Grey Scale 2 offers a more restricted form of grey scaling, such that only a maximum of four dot-patterns are used for any image in any printer graphics mode. This option is in fact designed to match the A2024 monitor display.

Color is only applicable if you have a colour printer. If selected, instead of varying the dot-patterns to reproduce a screen image in shades of grey, colour commands are sent to the printer to change the colour of the ink used.

Threshold

This option is only applicable to black and white printing and as a rule seems to be ignored if you are printing either in colour or grey scales. The Threshold setting determines which colours on the screen are printed as white and which as black. The setting is made using a slider gadget which can be dragged to give settings from 1 to 15. The higher the Threshold setting the more colours are printed in black assuming that Image is set to Positive. Therefore with a low Threshold setting (say 1 or 2) only the darkest colours on the screen are printed as black.

If Image is set to negative then the reverse is the case.

Density

Density, works on a scale of 1 to 7 and effectively sets how dark your printed image will be when printed. The lower the density setting, the faster the image will print as less dots are used, resulting in a lighter image. The higher the density setting, the more dots are used to create the image, the longer it takes to print and the darker – more dense – the image appears.

Note that there are many factors involved in using Density. For example, the EpsonX printer driver only supports six densities – therefore you can't use all seven settings! These and other subjects are more fully covered in *Mastering Amiga Printers*.

GraphicDump

If you are looking to produce screen dumps from the Workbench then the easiest option is to use GraphicDump which can be found in the Tools drawer on the Extras disk. This program will print the front-most image on the screen, ie the window at the front, to the printer when you double-click on the icon. However, as the window at the front of the screen when you double-click on the GraphicDump icon will almost certainly be the one containing GraphicDump there is about a 10 second delay before the program seeks the front window to allow you to bring it to the front.

The print to the printer takes place in real-time. That is, GraphicDump does not, at the allocated time, take a look at the front most screen and record it to memory for subsequent downloading to the printer, instead it looks at the screen and prints a line at a time.

This basically means that, unless you want to get some weird and wonderful effects, you should leave the screen well alone until the image has been printed.

The type of image produced by GraphicDump is affected by the settings of the Printer and PrinterGfx Preference editors. Equally it is possible to define the size of the dump produced by assigning the correct Tool Type to the GraphicDump information window.

Insider Guide #50: Using GraphicDump.

The size of a graphic dump can be set to four predetermined sizes called TINY, SMALL, MEDIUM and LARGE.

To set a size, select the GraphicDump icon by clicking on it once and then select the

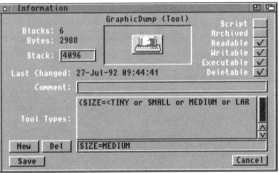

Information option from the Icons menu. This will display the Information screen.

Click on the New gadget to ungrey the string gadget. Click in the gadget and then at the keyboard enter: SIZE=

Follow this by the option required. In the above example SIZE is set so that SIZE=MEDIUM. Select Save to preserve your setting.

20

The Amiga can display text on the screen in a whole number of ways. Just experimenting can be fun but also highly informative.

It also throws up a new library of jargon to learn. Do just that and have a fontastic time as well playing with the editors!

```
┌─┬──────────────────────────────────────┬───┬──┐
│▫│ Select Workbench Icon Text        │⌐│⌐│
├─┴──────────────────────────────────────┴───┴──┤
│ LetterGothic                          11      │
│ opal                                  13      │
│ ruby                                  15      │
│ sapphire                              18      │
│ times                                 24      │
│ topaz                                         │
├──────────────────────────────────┬────────────┤
│ times                             │ 11         │
└──────────────────────────────────┴────────────┘
         Text:  █  ███  
         Field: █  ███  
         Mode:  [↵] Text+Field
```

*O*ne of the major areas where the Amiga has developed with the release of Workbench 2 as featured on the A600 is in the area of fonts – the various ways in which you can display type on the screen and on printer output. This is a vast and complicated subject and an important one. But I can only begin to touch the surface of this huge topic here.

The study of fonts is a science in itself and comes under the heading of *typography*. With the increasing use of computers such as the Amiga in publishing, especially in the application of programs such as desktop publishing, typographical terms have wormed their way into the ever expanding world of computer jargon. More terms for you to learn!

Unless you are into typography you have probably never paid much attention to the style of the text (type) that you read. In fact, there are many hundreds (and probably thousands) of styles of type and these are called fonts. For instance, the very text you are reading now is typeset in a font called New Aster. For shorthand we might normally say: the text is set in New

Aster. The two most common fonts in use are called Times and Helvetica and these are often seen in newspapers. Check out your daily! By default the Amiga uses a font called Topaz.

One thing you will have noticed is that the printed word comes in many sizes – type sizes are normally measured in their own system called *points*. A point is very fractionally over 1/72nd of an inch, although it is normally referred to as being 1/72nd of an inch. Therefore a font that is one inch high is said to be 72 points high.

Although there are many different fonts to choose from they can all be divided into two basic categories which are called serif and sans serif fonts.

A serif font is one that is adorned with fancy edges, the most famous of which is Times. Helvetica does not have these extra bits and is an example of a sans (without) serif font. Although there are no hard and fast rules, by convention sans serif fonts are used for headlines and serif fonts for main text because they are easier on the eye. So, how do you know what fonts are serif and which are sans serif? Look at them!

The appearance of a font on your Amiga screen might well look very different to that which you get when you print out hard copy containing the same fonts. This is especially the case when printing from DTP style programs which have specialist printer drivers rather than those that simply dump the screen. The reason for this difference is that the Amiga's screen display does not correspond in a 1:1 ratio with the equivalent area on a printed page. The bottom line is that fonts on screen will appear about twice as high on the screen as they do in the printed copy.

In addition the resolution of your screen is about 25% that of a dot-matrix printer. As such the appearance of the font on screen looks very jagged and on larger type sizes takes on an almost pyramidic look. The printed font looks infinitely better. Bear these points in mind when you use fonts initially, with some experience you will get used to this.

Amiga Fonts

Your Amiga is supplied with a Fonts disk and this contains additional fonts – in fact it contains all your fonts except those built into the Amiga system, ie the font called Topaz. The original Commodore fonts are all named after semi-precious stones, Emerald, Diamond and Garnet. These are all bitmapped fonts, that is

Insider Guide #51: Font types and Font sizes.

There are many types and styles of fonts. The way in which a font looks is called its typeface and there are many hundreds of different styles.

The main text in this book is set in New Aster.

The size of text is defined by a unit of measurement called a point.

This font is New Aster

This font is Lucida

This font is Bodoni Bold

This font is Palatino

This is 10 point text

This is 12 point text

This is 14 point text

Generally text is normally set either in 10 point or 12 point.

Fonts can be broadly categorised as serif or sans serif. Serif fonts such as Times have ornate edges while sans serif ones do not.

Sans serif means without serifs.

This is Times a serif Font

This is Helvetica a sans serif font

to say, they are stored on disk in the form of pixels which are literally dumped to the printer when they are needed. This is efficient in the fact that it is relatively quick but it does not result in a nice looking font. This is especially the case when the font is scaled up. The software simply fills in the gaps which leads to a very jagged edged font – all the bits of the bitmap simply get bigger!

A new technology (to the Amiga) has been the introduction of outline fonts from Compugraphic called *Intellifont*. The data for these fonts are stored in the form of a set of coordinates which plot out the characters of each letter – a mathematical representation of the font if you like. The great thing about this is that they can be printed in any size without loss of quality. The outline mathematics are simply scaled accordingly. While the final output is massively improved, the overhead is that the fonts take longer to produce. The trade-off is your's to decide upon. Outline fonts on the Fonts disk include CGTimes, CGTriumvirant and LetterGothic.

You can use any of the standard Commodore fonts simply by copying them into the Fonts directory on the Workbench disk. In release 2.1 of Workbench there is room to do this, however in version 2.04 there is very little space on the Workbench disk unless you remove some of the files you are not using. Because the Amiga uses bitmap fonts for the screen display you cannot use the Intellifonts straight off – you must create a bitmap set first using Fountain.

Once you have installed a new set of fonts you must first run the FixFonts utility to ensure that the Amiga knows about them – more on this shortly.

Extra Fonts

On the Workbench 2.1 disk there is plenty of room for you to add extra fonts simply by copying them across from the Fonts disk. With Workbench 2.0 (ie 2.04/2.05), if you have not added any extra files onto your Workbench disk you might just have enough room to copy an additional Amiga font onto it. If you are totally full – and you will need about 15K of free space to move a font such as Emerald across – you could try removing some of the less vital Workbench files.

You can copy any of the fonts supplied onto your Workbench disk, including the bitmap versions of the Intellifonts outlined above – once converted with Fountain that is. The limiting factor is the space available on your Workbench disk.

There are no icons associated with the fonts on the Fonts disk and therefore you will either need to use the Shell to move files or force icons to be displayed by using the Show All Files option from the Workbench menu. Files should be copied into the Fonts directory on the Workbench disk.

If you examine the Emerald directory you will find that it contains two files, both with numbers as names, 17 and 20. These are the font files and relate to their size. To install Emerald, copy the Emerald drawer across into the Fonts directory on the Workbench disk. You will also need to copy across the appropriate .font file. If you catalogue the Fonts disk you will see that there is a file called:

```
emerald.font
```

which is the one that must be copied into the Fonts directory on the Workbench disk. Once the fonts are in position you need to open the System drawer and double-click on the FixFonts to install them into the system and make them ready for use. Remember that for each font you need:

The font directory

The .font file

Insider Guide #52: Using Font Preferences.

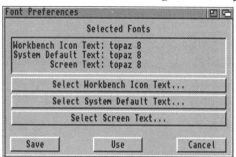

The Font Preferences editor displays current system settings and gives access to the three regions where you can edit the Amiga's font use to suit your own needs.

Use the scrolling windows to select the font you wish to use and the size.

It is possible to change both the colour of the text and in also the background colour for icon text using the palettes provided.

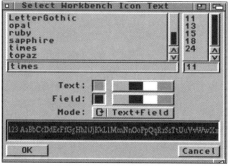

Use the menus to save your selections as preset options.

Font Prefs

In the Prefs drawer (Extras 2.1 or Workbench 2.0) you will find a preferences editor called Font. The Font editor has a simple role to play. It allows you to select the fonts that you wish to use on the Amiga, more specifically the font that is used to produce the menus, window names, icon names and so forth. Having said that the results that can occur if you decide to change the system font can be pretty awful. Topaz was designed for the job it docs and it does it very well.

When the Font Preferences editor window opens – under Workbench 2.1 – it displays a simple screen that defines the current settings and provides three button gadgets from which you can select either:

> Workbench Icon Text
>
> System Default Text
>
> Screen Text

When one of these is selected a further window appears showing a list of the fonts installed in your system along with some text showing how the selected font looks.

Under Workbench 2.0 this preview screen does not display, instead both are combined into a single window but the operation is identical apart from that fact.

The actual text affected by each of the three font window options is as follows:

Workbench icon text:
> This is the text below the icons in Workbench windows.

Screen text:
> This is the text that appears in menus, title bars, requesters and so forth.

System default text:
> The text that is displayed in output windows.

So, for example, to set the Workbench icon text to Emerald 17, first select the Workbench text icon button then locate and click on Emerald from the list of installed fonts. Finally select the size from the second list. Once you have selected these items from the lists you should get a preview of the text in the alphabet box. If you are happy select the OK button. You can use the menus provided to save font selections as Presets in the normal way (2.1 only).

When dealing with Workbench icon text you can specify the colour of the text and also of the field, ie the space in which the text is displayed. You can then use the Text and Field colour palettes which are displayed with the font list to select the colours required.

Of course, it should go without saying that it's not a good idea to use text and field colours that are the same. Then again, if you want to confuse a friend who has an Amiga...

21

There are a number of highly useful tools which you are yet to encounter.

You can read, write and format MS-DOS disks as though they were Amiga disks, adjust how sweet your A600 sounds and check your chips!

```
Input Preferences

                           Mouse
          Mouse Speed:    3  [        ]
          Acceleration:      [   ]
   Double-Click Delay:   75  [        ■]
      [ Show Double-Click  > ] [       ]
      [ Test Double-Click  > ] [       ]
```

*I*n this chapter we'll look at some of the utilities that are available on your Amiga A600, that are of use and which we haven't encountered yet. These include several features which are only available with release 2.1 of Workbench and not versions 2.04 and 2.05. You can check which version you have simply by looking at your Workbench disk. It will say either Workbench 2.1 or Workbench 2.0.

ShowConfig

This Tool is available in version 2.1 and 2.05 of Workbench and when double-clicked it opens a window which displays information about the Amiga you are using. This information is generally called the configuration – thus the term Show Configuration.

The details are banded under five headings. Processor lists the type of CPU you have installed and this is followed by the names of the major microchips. These chips are called custom chips because they were developed especially by Commodore for the Amiga and they have been given girls names – Agnus and Denise.

As you may be aware Commodore regularly updates its software such as Workbench and you can get information about the versions of the various files you are using from the Vers line. This is followed by details on the RAM memory you are using and finally any boards that you have fitted (such as memory upgrades) are listed.

If you ever experienced any problems with your Amiga, always run this tool first and make a note of the configuration before seeking expert advice from your dealer. Chances are it may help him solve a problem for you!

CrossDOS

CrossDOS is a commodity and only present in version 2.1 and later of Workbench. It allows you to use your Amiga to read and write MS-DOS format disks. Thus you could, for example, use your Amiga at home as a wordprocessing station and copy the information onto a PC disk for use in school or office. Of course, you are not only limited to PCs. Virtually all computers now available have the ability to read and write PC disks, therefore it can also be used as a transfer platform to exchange information between any two computer systems.

A point to bear in mind though is that CrossDOS offers only minimal file exchange capabilities and it is therefore up to you to ensure that the source and destination software are compatible. For example, if exchanging text you should save in ASCII format unless using a similar wordprocessor such as Protext on the Amiga and Protext on the PC.

Before you can use CrossDOS you must first install it and this involves a simple decision – what floppy disk drive are you going to use. The decision may be made for you if you only have an internal drive. If you have an extra external drive you could use this. At the end of the day your choice is only one of convenience because even after you have designated a disk drive as the MS-DOS disk drive you can still use it as an Amiga disk drive.

You will need to have your Workbench 2.1 and Extras 2.1 disks available. Copy the DOS Driver from the Extras 2.1:Storage/DOSDrivers to the Workbench2.1:Devs/DOSDrivers drawer. Once there, every time

Insider Guide #53: Installing CrossDOS.

Open the DOSDrivers drawers in the Devs and Storage drawers of the Extras2.1 and Workbench2.1 disks respectively.

To set the internal disk drive to read MS-DOS disks copy the PC0 icon across.

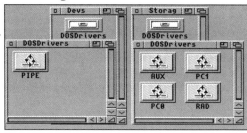

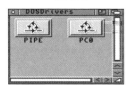

To set an external disk drive (DF1) to read MS-DOS disks copy the PC1 file across.

When the Amiga is rebooted it will be capable of read MS-DOS disks in the designated drive.

Alternatively double-click on the icon required to give you instance access to CrossDOS.

Clicking on the CrossDOS commodity icon displays its window where some basic text filtering and translation is possible by clicking on the relevant gadgets.

your Amiga is booted it will automatically allow the disk drive to be used to read a MS-DOS disk.

When a MS-DOS disk is inserted into the drive it will first appear as a bad disk icon but will then be duplicated on the Workbench showing its volume name.

MS-DOS format disks can be accessed from the AmigaShell using most of the standard AmigaDOS commands. The disk may be referred to by its volume name using the normal convention or by use of the device name.

For example, if the internal disk drive was made MS-DOS compatible and a disk called PCDISK was inserted you could catalogue its directory in one of two ways:

```
DIR PCDISK:
```

or:

```
DIR PC0:
```

The Commodities drawer contains the CrossDOS icon which when run will display the CrossDOS commodities window.

SetMap

Under Workbench 2.1 it is a simple matter to install keymaps – you just ensure that the correct keymap icons are placed in the Keymaps drawer in the Devs directory on the Workbench disk and use the Input Preferences Editor to select the required keyboard type from the scrolling list. However, things are not so straightforward if you are using release 2.04 or 2.05 of Workbench. This section explains what to do if you are using either of these versions of Workbench.

First of all the correct keymap file must be copied to the Keymaps drawer located in the Devs drawer of the Workbench disk. To do this proceed as follows:

1. Open the Workbench window and select Show All Files from the Window menu.

2. Scroll through the window and locate the Devs drawer. Open this and close the Workbench window.

3. Open the Keymaps window and close the Devs window.

4. Insert the Extras disk and select Show All Files from the Window menu.

5. Open the Devs drawer and close the Extras disk window.

6. Open the keymaps window and close the Devs window.

You will now have two Keymaps windows displayed on the screen, one from the Workbench disk (which may contain the gb icon if you installed this earlier) and one from the Extras disk which contains the various keymaps.

7. Locate the keymap of your choice and drag this across into the Workbench keymaps window.

As this stage you may have to do a bit of disk swapping if you have a single drive. If you have a dual drive system then you should have the Workbench disk in one drive and the Extras disk in the other. Once this is done you can close the windows.

With the keymap in place it is now necessary to set the correct Tool Type. The subject of Tool Types is discussed in Chapter 16, however for the sake of completeness this is how you do it.

Insider Guide #54: Setting the Keymap under 2.1.

Under Workbench 2.1 the keymap in use can be selected through the Input Preferences editor.

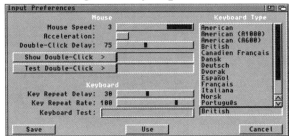

When opened the editor displays a list of keymaps available. To make a keymap available it must be copied from the Keymaps drawer in the Storage drawer (Extras2.1 disk) into the Keymaps drawer of the Devs drawer on the Workbench2.1 disk.

Simply double-click on the keymap required and then use Save to make the keymap selected available at all times or select Use to make it available until the next reboot.

Open the System drawer and select the Setmap icon by clicking on it once. Then, from the Icons menu, select the Information option to display the Information window. Locate the New button in the bottom left-hand corner of the window and select this. The text gadget to the right will cease to be greyed out. Now type the following:

KEYMAP=gb

where gb is the keymap you copied across – gb in this case being Great Britain. Press Return and the newly typed information will appear in the Tool Types window. Select the Save button and the process is completed.

If you ever wish to change the keymap again, proceed as already outlined and then simply edit the Tool Type setting by clicking on the KEYMAP option at which point it will be copied into the text gadget and is accessible to be edited.

Sound Prefs

In version 2.1 of Workbench a Sound Preferences Editor is introduced. This allows you to define what sort of noise your Amiga makes by default and also allows you to use sampled sound as well. Sampled sound is sound that you might have recorded using the Amiga.

Insider Guide #55: Using the Sound editor.

To set a new sound first ensure that the Make Sound gadget is ticked.

Drag the sliders to set the Volume, Pitch and Length required.

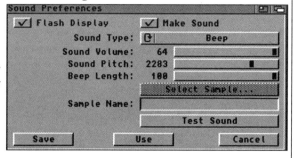

Click on the Sound Type gadget to set Sampled Sound. Double-click on the Select Sample button to display the Select IFF Sampled Sound file requester to locate the desired sample.

A sound can be tested at any point by clicking on the Test Sound button.

Sounds can be saved using the Save As option present in the Project menu.

Some software uses the Sound capabilities of the Amiga to signal certain stages in an operation. For example, disk copying programs will normally make the Amiga beep and perhaps flash the screen when they have completed their task. Equally, the system itself will occasionally throw up a beep when an error occurs. The sound of the beep can be defined using the Sound Preferences editor.

The editor is easy to use and by this stage you should feel quite happy with its layout and to experiment with it. By default most of the gadgets are greyed out and to access the full range you will need to check the Make Sound gadget.

Dragging the various slider gadgets allows you to define Volume, Pitch and Length while clicking on Test Sound will allow you to hear what effect your fiddling has had.

As with WBPattern preferences you can save Sounds in the same way using the menus provided. Ensure that the Create Icons? option is ticked in the Settings Menu and then select the Save As option from the Project menu. This will display a standard File Requester screen which, by default, puts saved Sounds in the Presets drawer.

Sampled sounds saved in IFF format can also be used and played in place of a beep. To utilise this click on the cycle gadget to move Beep on to Sample Sound and then double-click on the Sampled Sound button. This will display a file requester window through which you can locate the sampled sound you require.

A sound can be brought into immediate use by closing the editor window using the Use button. If the Save button is used the sound becomes the default one and will be used until changed again. Any sound saved in the Presets drawer can be invoked simply by double-clicking on its icon.

22

Juggling more than one ball at a time is difficult, but rewarding when mastered!

Your A600 can juggle programs and processes like a natural.

Here's how.

*O*ne of the major features of the Amiga is that it has multi-tasking capabilities. Multi-tasking is the ability to run several programs at once – where each program is seen by the Amiga as a task to do – hence the terminology. A task needn't be a commercial program or indeed one that you have written, a task can be any process that can be carried out by the Amiga, for instance, the formatting of a disk, or the running of two Shells.

Tasks started by AmigaDOS are called *processes*. This distinction may seem trivial, but it is vital that you understand at least the naming conventions at this point. The ability of your Amiga to multi-task effectively will depend, to some extent, on the amount of memory installed. Each process is, by nature, going to require a certain amount of memory, therefore the more processes that are started the more memory is required. For instance, a 1Mb Amiga is capable of running several 100K programs, but clearly an Amiga that has, say, 2Mb of memory will be able to double the amount of similar sized processes that it can run. Simple math really!

Although it may seem as though AmigaDOS is running several programs at once, it would be more correct to say that it is running them together. The microprocessor inside the Amiga is only capable of carrying one instruction at a time. However, the illusion of being able to run several at once is created by employing the speed of the microprocessor to run a bit of each process one after the other. For example, if three processes were running, the Amiga would run a bit of process one, then a bit of process two and then a bit of process three. Having serviced all three processes it would start the loop again by running a bit of process one. And all of this is happening at a staggeringly fast speed in order to provide the illusion.

Of course when a large number of processes are running, the time it takes for the operating system to get back to the first process becomes perceptible, and the computer seems to slow down.

However, this only applies when you run processes that require to be continually *run* by the operating system and, in particular, games and graphic demonstrations. Some programs are more docile in operation – they go to sleep, as it were, and don't use any processor time until something wakes them up. For example, memory permitting, running five or six wordprocessors at once would not have any apparent drag on the system.

The usefulness of multi-tasking will become more apparent as you use it. Being able to print a long file on an attached printer and to continue working at the computer is something many systems are unable to achieve. To your A600 it comes naturally!

Single Window

You may have already discovered that it is possible to start several programs at once from Workbench. If you haven't already tried this, now would be a good time! Open the Utilities drawer on your Workbench disk. Among other things, you should find: Say and Clock. Double-click on each of these in turn and, hey-presto, they both appear! You can even type text into the Say while the clock is running.

In a programming environment it is normally better to run the programs directly from the Shell window itself. This can be done simply by typing the name of the program to be run as an AmigaDOS command.

CD Utilities

Clock

The program will run but the Shell window will not respond to any further commands typed. The command RUN is used to overcome this obstacle, allowing programs to be set into motion and then returning the Shell prompt allowing the command line interface to be used as per normal. The syntax of the command is:

RUN <program>

Try running the Clock program once again using the RUN command as follows:

RUN Clock

The Clock program is set in motion and the prompt returns to the Shell window. The other programs can be launched in the same way – but don't do this just yet.

At this stage you will still be able to type in the Shell window with the Clock running in the background. A special feature designed into the Amiga allows this to happen. However, it is more common for a program to switch to its own window when it's launched.

If this were not done, you'd end up having to activate the window (by clicking in it) before you could interact with it. Clock is a special case which normally doesn't require any help from you. The other two programs mentioned need something from you – so they switch their windows *on* when they start. This means that as soon as the window for say, Calculator, opens, the Shell window becomes deactivated and you get stuck in the middle of a sentence.

The Commodity AutoPoint provides an answer, but it can cause as many problems as it solves. At this stage, therefore, don't use AutoPoint just yet. Now type the following:

RUN Say

The Shell window title bar changes colour from blue (selected) to grey (unselected). Just click back in the Shell window again to get control back.

Note that each time a new process is run a number is printed within square brackets. This is called the process number and AmigaDOS uses it to keep track of the programs it has running. There is no limit to the number of processes you can have running at any one time other than those constraints imposed by speed and memory.

Process Status

Now, if you have several or many processes running together it is useful to be able to keep track of them. AmigaDOS provides the STATUS command for this purpose and when typed this will provide information about the process currently running from a Shell window. If you open a Shell window and run the SAY and CLOCK programs, typing the command STATUS will produce the following output (the order may be different):

```
Process 1: Loaded as command: say

Process 2: Loaded as command: ConClip

Process 3: Loaded as command: Workbench

Process 4: Loaded as command: status

Process 5: Loaded as command: clock
```

This lists the various processes that are running from that particular Shell window. The *process* number is the number allocated to the process when it was launched.

If you want to find out the status of a particular command you can do so by specifying the option COMMAND and the name of the command itself. For instance if CLOCK was running then typing the following AmigaDOS:

```
STATUS COMMAND CLOCK
```

would print the number of the processes to which CLOCK was assigned when it was run.

Quitting Process

To be able to quit a process rather relies on the software running the process recognising the fact that you want to. This is not as daft as it may first seem as many programs are written in such a way that means that they cannot be interrupted at all. If a program is running in its own Shell window, and is written to allow interruption, then selecting the window and typing one of the following will halt the program:

```
<CTRL-C>
<CTRL-D>
<CTRL-E>
<CTRL-F>
```

For programs running from one window the command BREAK can be used. The syntax for BREAK is:

BREAK <process> <option>

For example to stop process number three use:

BREAK 3 ALL

Points In Mind
Running several programs at once is fine, so long as the majority of them can get on with the job without requiring continual input from you. Remember that your Amiga has just the one keyboard and all processes have to share this. Having to supply keyboard input continually to various programs can become a pain. If you need to, remember to select the window running the process first.

It is dangerous to use multi-tasking programs which require continual access to disks, and in single drive systems it can be suicidal. A situation will invariably arise where a process requests a disk, which is supplied, only to have another process request a second disk. Even without the wrist pain created, the disks will invariably become corrupted. On dual drive systems two processes can be made to use respective drives but the process of reading the information from the disk surfaces can, in certain circumstances, become slow and laborious.

**From the malicious to the mundane, viruses are
both fascinating and painful.**

**Only a very fortunate A600 user will never
encounter a virus. Are you that lucky or should you
take out the insurance of reading this chapter?**

```
□ | VirusX 2.10 by Steve Tibbett
      Disks Checked: 1
   Disks Installed: 0

      Viruses Found:
   SCA          : 0
   Byte Bandit  : 0
   North Star   : 0
   Byte Warrior : 0
   Revenge      : 0
```

With the computer has come the computer virus, and
with the Amiga has come its own specific viruses. A
virus is something that your Amiga can catch and,
just like the multitude of viruses that you and I might catch,
their severity ranges from annoying to software lethal. They are
a very real threat but provided you follow a set of basic principles you can avoid catching them. And if you do fall foul of one
or more, you should be able to find a cure.

The word virus derives from the 16th Century Latin for slime
or a poisonous liquid. In modern terms, it belongs to any of a
vast group of sub-microscopic DNA nuclei dressed in a protein
coat. These simple organisms are one of the most basic forms
of life, only capable of living and reproducing within the cells
of other animals and plants. Many are pathogenic, creating
symptoms ranging from mild discomfort to death. Computer
viruses ape their protein-coated namesakes very closely. So
closely in fact, some pundits have speculated that they consti-
tute a simple form of life. Indeed a recommended read is

Trojan by James Follett which exploits this topic in a thoroughly enjoyable novel. However, that is a philosophical avenue best explored during a late night discussion over several glasses of an intoxicating substance.

As I have already said computer viruses are like human viruses, in the sense that they infest the host and pass themselves on through a point of contact. On the computer the point of contact is disks, so when a disk comes from an external source (a friend, a magazine, a PD house, a software company), there is a risk that there will be a virus on that disk. Having said that, magazines, PD houses and software companies are very, very conscientious about their disk production and it is extremely unlikely that you will catch a virus in this way – though the possibility remains. Dodgy sources are the more likely culprits. A disk from a friend of a friend's brother's sister is a dodgy source!

A computer virus is nothing more than a computer program written by a devious mind. The problem is the devious mind of the writer can be quite brilliant and you may not know you have a virus for some time. Some are time coded so that they openly appear at certain times or dates and some might only appear when you try to do a certain task – such as print a file or copy a file. Some are mega awful and go as far as erasing the contents of your disk. Some are simply mischievous and say they are wiping your hard disk only to return a few minutes later saying *fooled you!*

Of course this can all lead to an unmitigated state of paranoia. Your Amiga might well crash for a host of other reasons – out of memory, a poor piece of software, incompatibility – not for just playing host.

Once you put the infected disk into your computer, the virus spreads into the system, in other words the virus program jumps ship and copies itself into your machine and then infects any other disk you put into the computer by copying itself onto it. If you pass any disks onto your friends then they put the virus on their machine, and so it goes on. Do not underestimate the potential of viruses. Some can even survive soft-resets so that you need to turn your Amiga off before you can sort things out.

So you need to be vigilant. Every time you get a disk, check it using one of the many virus detection programs available and detailed later on.

The Strain of it

There are several distinct strains of computer virus – variants of the way the infection (replication) code is written and each has a name. As can be seen from this, viruses are ostensibly simple to write, which is why there are so many around:

Limpet

Often called the bootblock or boot sector virus. The term Limpet derives from the way the virus adheres to the bootblock of infected disks. These are the simplest viruses of them all – and usually the easiest to catch. These were also the first viruses to appear on the Amiga.

The very first Amiga Limpet came courtesy of Swiss Crackers Association or SCA – no prizes for guessing: pirates! Bootblock viruses consist of a small section of code which loads a disk's boot sectors when the computer is booted from an infected disk. Every time a new (write-enabled) disk is inserted, the virus writes itself back to the new disk thus infecting it. Depending on the type of Limpet, some write themselves back during soft resets, others to every uninfected disk inserted.

Doppleganger

This works by replacing the code of an original program completely with its own. Next it moves the code of the original program somewhere else on the same disk and gives it a blank name. When the original program is called, the virus runs (doing its dirty work) then exits by launching the real program. Sounds complex? Not at all – three simple AmigaDOS calls can be used to do this. BSG9 was an early example of this type and can be identified by the tell-tale blank file it leaves in the DEVS directory of the infected disk. The AmigaDOS' LIST command shows it up – DIR does not. If found, BSG9 is usually the first command in the S:Startup-sequence and has a bytesize of 2608 when listed.

Trojan Horse

Sometimes just called a Trojan, this type has yet to crop up on the Amiga in large numbers for reasons which will shortly be revealed. Trojans get their name from the Greek fable of the Trojan (or wooden) horse.

As the story goes, the Greeks bluffed the Trojans by leaving a wooden horse outside the gates of Troy. The Trojans dragged the horse inside, and at nightfall the Greeks hidden inside the beast crept in under cover of darkness and murdered the Trojans in their beds.

In the same way, a Trojan virus is a computer program, usually placed in the Public Domain not by Greeks, but still with a very sharp sting in its belly. The reason why real Trojans are rare is because they take some skill to implement. The only way they will spread is if the program hiding the stinger is useful enough for lots of people to use. And once the Trojan is uncovered, everyone stops using it. For this reason Trojans use a time-bomb technique whereby they only activate after they have been used a set number of times or, sometimes, on a certain date. Most Amiga Trojans are genuine programs infected by a Parasite – see below.

Parasite or Linkvirus

Also called Worm, Zombie, Lycanthrope, and Vampire. These bloodsuckers are the scourge of utility software and generally a real pain in the Startup-sequence. Like real vampires they duplicate by attaching themselves to other programs. The problem with parasites is they turn genuine software into Trojans by locking onto their code and transferring across onto all and sundry. Like Trojans, Parasites are tricky to implement so there are less around. Unlike the Limpets, they multiply between disks and across directories at an alarming rate. Also they're very tricky to catch without software specifically designed for the purpose – Peter Cushing never had it this tough.

Symptoms

There are two mainstream effects of virus infection: destructive and nuisance. Neither are very pleasant – some viruses exhibit both.

Silly messages Software piracy is theft..., AmigaDOS presents: The IRQ Virus, Something wonderful has happened and so on. The only wonderful thing that could happen to the persons responsible for these gems would be the spontaneous combustion of their Amigas.

Reversed keys The two Amiga keys, for example, suddenly become transposed.

Lock outs The whole machine stops accepting keyboard input – but everything else appears to be working normally.

Obscene mouse Pointers
> I kid you not – is nothing sacred?

Random trashing of files
> Has the effect of causing programs to suddenly crash without warning, corrupts data in pictures, music and text. Lamer Exterminator is known to have this effect.

Random trashing of disk files
> Difficult one to pin to a virus because it can also happen through wear and tear, badly stored disks and a whole host of other things. Likely sign of a virus if it starts suddenly.

Prevention

It only takes one slip to catch a virus because once the little beggars get onto a disk, they spread very quickly. This checklist covers the most important points.

1. No known virus can get past the write protection notch on a floppy. Never insert a write enabled disk unless something has to write to it. Better still keep data disks separate from program disks. If a virus gets into memory it can only spread to disks which are either (a) never booted or (b) don't contain any executable files.

2. Keep a Canary disk. This is a freshly formatted disk with a couple of commands and a Startup-sequence. If a Limpet tries to attach itself this disk will suddenly become bootable. A suite of programs to make Canary disks (and a lot more) is included with our sister book *Mastering AmigaDOS 2 Volume One*.

3. Get a disk of Virus killers from your friendly PD library and check every file and bootblock of every disk you get before attempting to boot them or run any of the programs contained therein.

4. Never, ever, use pirated software. This includes games, utilities and applications – it's a sure-fire way to catch a virus.

Viral Death

The only sure way to be virus free in this day of over 100 known viruses is to use a virus killer program. If you don't have a virus killer (and I strongly urge you to get one) then there is something you can do, although it is a little fiddly and doesn't help with all types of virus.

For the most part a virus will die if you switch the machine off. Obviously it still lives on the disks you have infected, but it won't linger in your machine if you switch off. And if you write protect a disk (put the little tab up so you can see a hole through the corner of the disk) the virus can't get onto it. Once you have switched off for about 30 seconds, turn back on and boot with your master Workbench disk (with its write protect tab on). Open a Shell, and insert the virus infected disk. Then install the bootblock (the area on the disk where the virus will normally linger) by typing:

    Install dfn:

where n is the drive you want to install. This prints a healthy bootblock over the infected one, so curing the problem. But when you inserted the infected disk to install it, the virus has infected your system again. But don't panic. Switch off the machine again, wait 30 seconds, and then reboot. You will now be virus free. Unless, that is, the virus you have is more sophisticated.

This method of killing viruses is only any good for viruses which live in the bootblock. Certain viruses, a type called the link virus, attach themselves to a healthy file and lie in wait, immune from being Installed. So, as I said at the start, the only certain way to catch these little beggars is to use a reputable virus killer. And choosing the right killer can be as important as having one at all.

For example there is a new kind of virus now, one called a Disk-Validator virus. There is only one type of this new virus at the moment, although there will probably be more by the time you read this, as it doesn't take long for people to rewrite these things. The thing is there is only one virus killer that detects and rubs out this particular new strain! So you have to choose wisely, if you want to be safe.

Warning: Some of your commercial software will have slightly out of the ordinary bootblocks on them. This is for copy protection, and if you kill them off with your virus killer, the program will not load. This is obviously undesirable as the program could be quite valuable, and although most software houses will replace a damaged disk with no questions, the fault is yours so they might not. Some virus killers recognise benign bootblocks, like those on a game disk, but some don't. Use a killer that knows about some of the more common benign bootblocks like the Electronic Arts variety for example. If in doubt, don't kill a block, especially on software you've bought.

The Killers

There are a great many virus killers on the market, and all of them are freely distributable. PD houses stock them, and usually you can guarantee that a virus killer disk at least will be free of viruses. (Obviously the guy who programmed the killer would take the trouble to kill the viruses on his own system!) There are many different types, and all of them are pretty good by now, having undergone many different revisions since the virus problem became apparent on the Amiga in around 1987.

However, at the time of writing two of the best available are ZeroVirus and Master Virus Killer, which both cover over 100 viruses and seem to be the most intelligent about which bootblocks and files they kill. As well as these programs to detect and kill a virus, if you think you have a problem, I'd recommend having a small killer in the C directory on your bootdisk, with a command to run it in your startup-sequence. I'd suggest CV, because it seems small enough to fit on a floppy as well as a hard drive.

Note: Most of the above killers are available on 17 Bit Software PD disk number 949. Master Virus Killer v2.1 is on 17 Bit disk 894.

The end of the road is nigh! But there is still so much to learn – what a wonderful world it is.

In this final chapter a brief introduction to just a few of the areas we have not covered in any depth. Then it's all up to you.

*T*he final chapter in this book has arrived and by now, if you have followed all of the examples, you should have got inside your Amiga and have a base knowledge of how to use its facilities both via the Workbench and through AmigaDOS.

However, there is still an awful lot I have not covered, but much of this you should now be able to explore with confidence. This final chapter is a very brief overview of some of the drawers and files we have not looked at. In particular:

The System Drawer

The Expansion Drawer

The Storage Drawer

The Preferences Drawer

The Locale Disk

System Drawer

The System drawer holds within it tools that, in general, have a direct effect on the way the Amiga system (ie the bit of the Amiga that makes it tick) works or are fundamental to the Amiga's operation – such as the Shell which we have already examined in some considerable depth.

Equally, several of the facilities provided are advanced in operation and for that reason you may wish to ignore them until you actually come to need to use them.

In addition to the Shell the function of FixFonts has been covered in Chapter 20. You run this when new fonts have been added and it informs the Amiga that they are there and can be used. This is often after the use of Fountain which allows you to create bitmap versions of Intellifonts for display on screen.

NoFastMem allows older Amiga programs to run on new machines. The early Amigas came with limited amounts of memory, therefore some very old programs work in a very limited way. However, as Amigas got better and their memory capabilities extended, programs got bigger and better. Except for those *very* old programs – when they are run they get upset with the extra memory as they don't expect to see it! The memory present in those long lost days was only graphics memory and this is in what those older programs expect to run. When NoFastMem is run it forces the Amiga to use only the available graphics memory. Running NoFastMem again re-enables all other memory. I can't believe anybody is still using such old programs. So, with that in mind, you can pretty much ignore this program.

In addition to AmigaDOS you can also program you Amiga in a number of different programming languages. In recent years ARexx has become increasingly popular as it allows you to customise existing programs (which use ARexx). RexxMast provides an interface that allows the ARexx language to be used. This is run as part of the Amiga's starting up process and is normally active, so if you should run it again it would be turned off.

Expansion

The Expansion drawer is a utility drawer and can be likened in a more limited respect to the operation of the WBStartup Drawer. The drawer is normally used to support the addition of peripheral devices – that is hardware that you plug into your

Amiga – for example, a scanner or a digitiser perhaps. You simply copy the software into the Expansion drawer and it does the rest. If you need to copy software here as part of installing a new purchase it will tell you to do so. Otherwise don't!

Storage Drawer

The Storage Drawer is introduced under Workbench 2.1 and is located on the Extras disk. It is here that files you are likely to need are kept to enable you to find and locate them readily. The Storage Drawer itself contains four drawers. DOSDrivers contains files relating to CrossDOS and other disk emulations; Keymaps contains the various international keyboard drivers; Monitors has files which allow you to add the software to run more advanced display systems; and Printers houses the various printer drivers. To use any of the files you simply copy them into the corresponding drawers in the Devs drawer on your Workbench startup disk.

Prefs Drawers

We have only looked at a few of the many Preference editors available to you. These really are great fun to explore and experiment with so don't hold back! The windows that they open should all be very familiar to you.

The IControl Preferences editor allows you to change and define various settings such as what command keys are used for certain operations and how long your Amiga will wait for a certain operation to happen before it gets fed up.

The Input Preferences editor allows you to fine tune the manner in which your mouse and keyboard operate. This basically boils down to the speed at which the Pointer moves across the screen in relation to movement of the mouse, how quick a double-click can be and how responsive keypresses on the keyboard are.

Sometimes when you use a monitor there is a small area around the edge of the screen that is unused – a *border* if you like. This region is called the overscan area and the purpose of the Overscan Preferences screen editor is to allow you to enlarge the size of your screen so that you can actually use this unused space!

The ScreenMode Preferences editor window allows you to select an appropriate screen mode for your Amiga. The modes available to you are listed in the scrollable Display Mode scroll gadget and the items listed here will depend on the monitor you are using and the monitor drivers you might have copied across from the Storage drawer (under Workbench 2.1).

Locale Disk

Under release 2.1 of Workbench an additional disk – the Locale Disk – is supplied, and the Prefs drawer on the Extras disk also contains an additional editor – the Locale Preferences editor.

The Locale disk contains the information needed to support the new international localisation offered by the Amiga from the launch of Workbench 2.1. Essentially it provides an easy way for applications to support various languages in the international markets that Commodore supports – the idea being that a software developer can write a single program that runs in any of the languages supported according to the user's preference.

The languages supported by Locale are:

- English
- German
- French
- Italian
- Danish

- Spanish
- Portuguese
- Swedish
- Norwegian
- Dutch

So, provided the application supports localisation, you can use it in any of the supported languages just by modifying the settings through the Locale Preferences editor.

Commodore may keep moving the location of their files but we keep keeping up with them!

Wherever a particular tool, font or data file may be on your disks, this guide will give you instant alphabetical access.

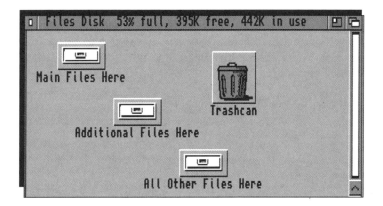

*T*he A600 and A600HD both come supplied with two different versions of Workbench. The early A600s were shipped with Workbench 2.04 – shown as Workbench2.0 on the disk set. The early A600HDs were supplied with Workbench 2.05, again this was shown as Workbench2.0 on the disk set.

More recent A600s and A600HDs have been supplied with Workbench 2.1. This later version of Workbench has a number of extras, several of which are outlined in this book. That said, for the major part, the two are virtually identical in operation and for you will not notice a great deal of difference in general use.

However, the position of certain files across the disk sets has changed. For instance, the Shell is in the root directory on Workbench 2.04/2.05 but in the System drawer in Workbench 2.1. Similarly most of the Preferences editors can be found on the Extras disk in 2.1 but on the Workbench disk in 2.04/2.05.

To enable you to locate a particular tool or project this appendix lists all of the files supplied on your Amiga Workbench 2.0 disk set and then again from the Workbench 2.1 disk set.

Each file is listed in alphabetical order and is followed by its directory location. This should enable you to locate a particular file quickly and efficiently. Note that all files are listed, not just those with icons. Access to these files can be via the Workbench Show All Files option or through the Shell itself.

For example, if you wished to locate the file Startup-sequence, locate the name in the list and see that it can be found in the S directory. Files that are listed without a directory name next to them can be found in the root of the Workbench2.0 disk. File names that have (Dir) next to them are in fact directories.

Workbench 2.0/Extras2.0 Disk Set

A

A2024	Extras2.0:MonitorStore
A2024.info	Extras2.0:MonitorStore
AddBuffers	Workbench2.0:C
AddMonitor	Workbench2.0:System
AddMonitor.info	Workbench2.0:System
asl.library	Workbench2.0:Libs
Assign	Workbench2.0:C
AutoPoint	Extras2.0:Tools/Commodities
AutoPoint.info	Extras2.0:Tools/Commodities
aux-handler	Workbench2.0:L
Avail	Workbench2.0:C

B

BindDrivers	Workbench2.0:C
BindMonitor	Workbench2.0:System
BindMonitor.info	Workbench2.0:System
Blanker	Extras2.0:Tools/Commodities
Blanker.info	Extras2.0:Tools/Commodities
Break	Workbench2.0:C
BRU	Extras2.0:Tools
BRUtab	Workbench2.0:S

C

C	Workbench2.0:Dir
CalComp_ColorMaster	Extras2.0:Devs/Printers
CalComp_ColorMaster2	Extras2.0:Devs/Printers
Calculator	Extras2.0:Tools
Calculator.info	Extras2.0:Tools
CBM_MPS1000	Extras2.0:Devs/Printers
cdn	Extras2.0:Devs/Keymaps

ch1 ....Extras2.0:Devs/Keymaps
ch2 ....Extras2.0:Devs/Keymaps
ChangeTaskPri Workbench2.0:C
CLI Workbench2.0:System
CLI.info Workbench2.0:System
ClickToFront Extras2.0:Tools/Commodities
ClickToFront.info Extras2.0:Tools/Commodities
clipboard.device Workbench2.0:Devs
Clock Workbench2.0:Utilities
Clock.info Workbench2.0:Utilities
CMD...Extras2.0:Tools
CMD.info Extras2.0:Tools
Colors Extras2.0:Tools
Colors.info Extras2.0:Tools
Commodities (Dir) Extras2.0:Tools
Commodities.info...................................Extras2.0:Tools
commodities.library...............................Workbench2.0:Libs
ConClip...Workbench2.0:C
Copy Workbench2.0:C
CPU Workbench2.0:C

D

d Extras2.0:Devs/Keymaps
Date Workbench2.0:C
Delete..Workbench2.0:C
Devs (Dir) Extras2.0:
Devs (Dir) Workbench2.0:
Devs/Keymaps (Dir) Workbench2.0:
Diablo_630 ....Extras2.0:Devs/Printers
Dir Workbench2.0:C
disk.info Extras2.0:
disk.info Workbench2.0:
DiskChange Workbench2.0:C
DiskCopy Workbench2.0:System
DiskCopy.info Workbench2.0:System
DiskDoctor Workbench2.0:C
diskfont.library Workbench2.0:Libs
Display..Workbench2.0:Utilities
Display.info Workbench2.0:Utilities
dk...Extras2.0:Devs/Keymaps
DPat Workbench2.0:S

E

e Extras2.0:Devs/Keymaps
Ed Workbench2.0:C
Ed-startup..Workbench2.0:S
Edit Workbench2.0:C
Env-Archive Workbench2.0:Prefs
EpsonQ..Extras2.0:Devs/Printers
EpsonX...Extras2.0:Devs/Printers
EpsonXOld Extras2.0:Devs/Printers

U

V

W

X

Workbench 2.1/Extras 2.1 Disk Set

A

E

F

W

X

We've taken you inside your A600, now comes the opportunity to take your computing a serious step further with our Mastering Series.

You'll be getting an idea by now where your interests lie and our interest is in providing the book to help you with your hobby.

*B*ruce Smith Books is dedicated to producing quality Amiga publications which are both comprehensive and easy to read. Our Amiga titles are being written by some of the best known names in the marvellous world of Amiga computing. If you have found that your Insider Guide informative and want to delve deeper into your Amiga then why not try one of our highly rated Mastering Amiga guides. In otherwords – if you enjoyed getting insider your Amiga, now is the time to master it!

Below you will find details of all our books in the Mastering Amiga range that are either currently available or due for publication. As an ideal follow-on to this title we would recommend *Mastering AmigaDOS Volume One* and *Mastering Amiga Workbench 2*, both of which delve deep inside both AmigaDOS and Workbench 2, far beyond what you have already learnt. Some of the material will be familar to you, but much more will come to life from these texts which are the most comprehensive available.

Titles Currently Available:

- Mastering Amiga Beginners
- Mastering AmigaDOS Volume One
- Mastering AmigaDOS Volume Two
- Mastering Amiga C
- Mastering Amiga Printers
- Mastering Amiga Workbench2
- Mastering Amiga System
- Mastering Amiga Assembler
- Mastering Amiga AMOS

Titles Coming Soon:

- Mastering Amiga ARexx
- Amiga Gamer Volume One
- Amiga A1200 Insider Guide

Brief details of these guides along with review segments are given below. If you would like a free copy of our catalogue Mastering Amiga News and to be placed on our mailing list then phone or write to the address below.

You can order a book simply by writing or using the simple tear our form to be found towards the end of this book.

Our mailing list is used exclusively to inform readers of forthcoming Bruce Smith Books publications along with special introductory offers which normally take the form of a free software disk when ordering the publication direct from us.

> Bruce Smith Books, PO Box 382, St. Albans, Herts, AL2 3JD
> Telephone: (0923) 894355 Fax: (0923) 894366

Note that we offer a 24-hour telephone answer system so that you can place your order direct by 'phone at a time to suit yourself. When ordering by 'phone please:

- Speak clearly and slowly
- Leave your full name and full address
- Leave a day-time contact phone number

- Give your credit card number and expiry date
- Spell out any unusual names

Note that we do not charge for P&P in the UK and we endeavour to dispatch all books within 24-hours.

Buying at your Bookshop

All our books can be obtained via your local bookshops – this includes WH Smiths which will be keeping a stock of some of our titles – just enquire at their counter. If you wish to order via your local High Street bookshop you wil need to supply the book name, author, publisher, price and ISBN number – these are all summarised at the very end of this appendix.

Overseas Orders

Please add £3 per book (Europe) or £6 per book (outside Europe) to cover postage and packing. Pay by sterling cheque or by Access, Visa or Mastercard. Post, Fax or Phone your order to us.

Dealer Enquiries

Our distributor is Computer Bookshops Ltd who keep a good stock of all our titles. Call their Customer Services Department for best terms on 021-706-1188.

Compatibility

We endeavour to ensure that all Mastering Amiga books are fully compatible with all Amiga models and all releases of AmigaDOS and Workbench.

Mastering Amiga Workbench 2

The Workbench is one of the most important aspects of the Amiga, yet so few users really understand how to use it to its full potential. From it you can access virtually all of the Amiga's functions and determine how your computer will operate from the moment it is switched on. With the advent of Workbench 2, running under the much enhanced AmigaDOS 2, the options open to the Workbench users are greater than ever before.

In this book Bruce Smith explains everything you will want to know about the Workbench version 2.x, using screen illustrations throughout for ease of reference. The book is geared towards all types of users, whether you have a single floppy disk or a hard disk to operate from.

Starting from first steps the book explains the philosophy of the Workbench and how it ties in with your Amiga. It then moves on to describe the best way to perform basic housekeeping tasks such as disk copying, file transfer and how to customise your own Workbench disks for different occasions and requirements.

The author works his way through each of the menu options with full descriptions of their use, providing many hints, tips and tricks en route. By this stage you will already be an accomplished Workbench user, but as the books enters its final stages you will make the transition to expert status as areas such as Preferences, Tools and Commodities are fully explained.

In effect *Mastering Amiga Workbench 2* provides you with a complete guide to your Workbench and Extras disks in an easy to read style guaranteed to upgrade you to full proficiency on your Amiga.

Mastering AmigaDOS 2

Our 700-page plus dual volume set covers all versions of AmigaDOS from 1.2, including 1.2, 1.3, 1.3.2 and 2.x. Volume One is a complete tutorial for AmigaDOS users, both beginners and experts alike. Volume Two is a detailed and comprehensive reference to all AmigaDOS commands.

Here's what the press said:

"If you're a complete beginner or unsure of a few areas, this book is an amazingly informative read." Amiga Format on Volume One

"As a reference book it's very useful. So far as I know there isn't any similar book...If you need to know how every AmigaDOS command works get this book...it is a definitive reference" Amiga Format on Volume Two.

"The Reference book that Commodore forgot to commission" Keith Pomfret of New Computer Express on Volume Two.

"The book can be strongly recommended...and even more strongly to those having difficulty getting to grips with its various commands. You won't find a better guide to, or a more useful book on, the Amiga than this" Micronet AmigaBASE.

"No other authors have investigated AmigaDOS with the thoroughness of Smith and Smiddy and every page provides useful information. Put off getting that new game, and buy this instead. You won't regret it." Micronet AmigaBASE.

And if you don't know if you need either or both books here is what Amiga Format suggested: "If Volume 1 is so good what is the point of having Volume 2? Volume 1 is a tutorial, it teaches you how to use AmigaDOS. Volume 2 is more of a manual."

Mastering Amiga Beginners

The Amiga has enjoyed a phenomenal success over recent years and is now recognised as one of the most powerful and sophisticated computers available. The appeal of the Amiga along with the vast range of programs available for it has made it the ideal machine for the ambitious beginner.

If you have recently purchased an Amiga of any type, or have had one for some time but now feel you are still not getting to grips with what lies behind that keyboard then this is definitely the book for you!

Written by Phil South, recognised as one of the most prolific and knowledgeable of Amiga authors, this book will take you step by step through every aspect of its use, from disks and disk drives to AmigaDOS and the extras available to it. It does so in a logical manner, introducing items as and when they are needed so as to become a powerful torchlight through the fog of computer jargon.

This book will not make you an expert in any one particular subject but it will provide you with a solid grounding to allow you to investigate those areas which appeal to you, either on your own or with another book from the growing Mastering Amiga series of publications.

But you don't have to take our word for it, here's a snippet or two from a review of the book that appeared in CU Amiga under the headline Beginners Bible.

"...this book is both a highly readable and entertaining introduction to the Amiga.....the book gives useful hints and tips rather than detailed instruction, and this works very well...An excellent introduction to the Amiga, and even at £20 it's an extremely worthwhile investment for the beginner."

Added to this if you order direct from us you can choose to receive a free disk of PD software. Choose from a Wordprocessor (including spell check) or a Games Compendium. State which when you order.

Mastering Amiga C

C is without doubt one of the most powerful programming languages ever created, and it has a very special relationship with the Commodore Amiga. Much of the Amiga's operating system software was written using C and almost all of the Amiga technical reference books assume some proficiency in the language.

Paul Overaa has been writing about C and the Amiga for as long as the machine has been in existence. He knows the Amiga-specific pitfalls that can plague the beginner, knows how to avoid them, and above all he knows about C. Best of all he's prepared to share that experience. The result is a book which is guaranteed to get the Amiga owner programming in C as quickly and as painlessly as possible.

This introductory text assumes no prior knowledge of C and covers all the major compilers, including Lattice/SAS and Aztec. What is more it also covers NorthC – the Charityware compiler – so that anyone who is interested in learning C can do so for just a few pounds. This book assumes no prior knowledge of C and features:

- Easy to follow tutorials

- All major C compilers

- Explanations of special Amiga C features

- Amiga problem areas

- Debugging and testing

Here's what CU Amiga thought of Mastering Amiga C: "This book has been written with the absolute novice in mind. It doesn't baffle with jargon and slang".

Writing in Amiga User International, Mike Nelson called Mastering Amiga C: "Very thorough, Paul Overaa has gone to considerable lengths to keep up to date with developments in the real world of C and the ANSI Standards...this book will go a long way to help you master C on your Amiga".

Mastering Amiga Printers

Next to the Amiga itself, your printer is the largest and most important purchase you're likely to make. It's surprising then, that so little help is available for those about to take this step, whether it be for the first time, or for the purpose of upgrading from an old, trusted but limited model to one of today's much more versatile and complex machines. The problem of course is that you can't take one home on trial to find out what it does.

Today's printers are extremely sophisticated and complex devices, with a wide range of capabilities, so it's all too easy to make a mistake at the stage of buying if you don't know what to look for, the right questions to ask and the sort of comparisons to make between similarly priced models from different manufacturers. Since a printer is such a large investment, quite possibly more expensive than the micro itself, choosing the right type and model for your needs is doubly important, because you'll have to live with your decision for a long time.

Unfortunately for the user, neither computer nor printer manufacturers see it as their responsibility to offer guidance or assistance to users in this important purchase.

Mastering Amiga Printers fills this gap perfectly. Making no assumptions about previous printer experience, the explanations begin with the basic principles of how printers work, including a run-down of the different types most commonly used with home and business micros.

After a comprehensive grounding in the abilities and methods of the different types of printer hardware you'll then learn how to install them in the Amiga. Preference selections and printer drivers are thoroughly explained for both Workbench One and Two, so you'll know not only which choices to make, but what they mean. There's also a thorough grounding in the direct use of printers from the command line, which you'll need if you want to write your own programs.

Additional chapters take a logical approach to trouble-shooting and routine maintenance, vital to the newcomer. These chapters include the sort of information and knowledge which is normally only available after long experience, the very thing the new user lacks. Mastering Amiga Printers is a must for every user who wants to get the best out of their Amiga and its printer.

Mastering Amiga System

A complete tutorial to Amiga System programming with copious examples. A basic knowledge of C is required but the book begins with short examples which only later build into full-scale programs, all of which are on the accompanying disk.

In dealing with a difficult subject, the author has avoided merely duplicating standard documentation. Instead he has entered on a journey through the different aspects of the Amiga's system, finding the safest and most effective routes to practical programs. Mastering Amiga System is an invaluable purchase for the Amiga programmer who wants to master the system software. Free disk.

Mastering Amiga Assembler

Although the 68000 processor series is well-documented, the use of assembly language to write efficient code within the unique environment of the Amiga is only now explained in this hands-on tutorial. Working with the Amiga's custom chips and system software are only two of the areas which will be appreciated by programmers wanting to generate machine code from the popular Amiga Assemblers, all of which are supported by the many code examples in this 416 page book.

Mastering Amiga AMOS

AMOS has revolutionised all forms of programming on the Amiga. What is more it has made it possible for every Amiga owner to create stunning sound and graphics with the absolute minimum of fuss. This book covers AMOS, and includes chapters on Easy AMOS and AMOS Professional. Just some of the topics covered include Windows, Text and Menus, Screens, Sprites and Bobs, Sprite X, CText and TOME, AMOS Compiler and 3D, Music and Sound and much more.

Mastering Amiga ARexx

Another great programming introduction from the wordprocessor of Paul Overaa – this book is a complete programming guide to the ARexx language. Packed full of examples for you to type in and try. Unleash this Amiga programming language now!

Summary Book Details

Mastering Amiga Beginners by Phil South
ISBN: 1-873308-03-5 – Price £19.95   320 pages. Now available.
FREE Wordprocessor or Games disk – please state preference.

Mastering AmigaDOS 2 Volume One – Revised Edition
by Bruce Smith and Mark Smiddy
ISBN: 1-873308-10-8 – Price £21.95   416 pages. Now available.
FREE Utilities disk.

Mastering AmigaDOS 2 Volume Two –Revised Edition
by Bruce Smith and Mark Smiddy
ISBN: 1-873308-09-4 – Price £19.95   368 pages. Now Available.

Mastering Amiga C by Paul Overaa
ISBN: 1-873308-04-6 – Price £19.95   320 pages. Now available.
FREE Programs Disk and NorthC Public Domain compiler.

Mastering Amiga Printers by Robin Burton
ISBN: 1-873308-05-1 – Price £19.95   336 pages. Now Available.
FREE Programs disk.

Mastering Amiga Workbench 2 by Bruce Smith
ISBN: 1-873308-08-6 – Price £19.95   320 pages. Now Available

Mastering Amiga System by Paul Overaa
ISBN: 1-873308-06-X – Price £29.95   398 pages. Now Available.
FREE disk.

Mastering Amiga Assembler by Paul Overaa
ISBN: 1-873308-11-6 – Price £24.95   416 pages. Now Available.
FREE disk.

Mastering Amiga AMOS by Phil South
ISBN: 1-873308-13-2 – Price £19.95   320 pages. Available Now.

Mastering Amiga ARexx by Paul Overa

ISBN: 1-873308-13-2 – Price £21.95   336 pages approx.
Available January 1993. FREE disk.

Note: Disks where indicated are supplied free only when ordered direct from Bruce Smith Books.

E&OE.

Z